Design for Health Care

The Butterworths Design Series for architects and planners

General Editor: Edward D. Mills, CBE, FRIBA, MSIA

Each book in the Butterworths Design Series takes an in-depth look at the design approach to a particular building type or building problem. Basic design philosophies are analysed in the context of the needs of the building user. Truly international in scope and coverage, the series draws on abundant worldwide examples of the best of modern design and planning.

All the books in the series have been specially commissioned from leading architects and specialists of worldwide repute. The Butterworths Design Series complements the publisher's *Planning* Series, and will be an invaluable reference for practising architects, schools of architecture and design, and departments of urban and rural development.

Other titles in the **'Design'** series

Design for Fire Safety
Eric W. Marchant

Design for Holidays and Tourism
Edward D Mills

Design for Leisure Entertainment
Anthony Wylson

Design for Shopping Centres
Nadine Beddington

Design for Sport
Gerald A. Perrin

Design for Health Care

Anthony Cox CBE, AA Dipl, FRIBA
and
Philip Groves FRIBA
Partners, Architects' Co-Partnership

Butterworths
London Boston Sydney Wellington Durban Toronto

First published 1981
© Butterworth & Co (Publishers) Ltd, 1981

**British Library Cataloguing in Publication
Data**

Cox, Anthony
  Design for Health Care.
  1. Health facilities – Design and construction
  I. Title   II. Groves, Philip
  725'.5   RA967   80–40735

  ISBN 0–408–00389–8

Typeset by Butterworths Litho Preparation Department
Printed and bound by Fakenham Press Ltd., Fakenham, Norfolk.

Foreword

Edward D. Mills, CBE, FRIBA, FSIA

Design for Health Care is the second book in the Butterworths Design Series and has been prepared by two partners of Architects Co-Partnership, whose wide experience in the field of health care is generally acknowledged.

The subject of health care is one which is being given increasing attention throughout the world, as developing nations realise the importance of preventative medicine as well as medical treatment. The effectiveness of such care is clearly apparent in the rapidly falling birth rate in many parts of the world and the greater life expectancy. It is of interest to note that in the 5th century in Britain, the life expectancy for males was 33, and for females 27. There was a time in recent years, when a centenarian in Britain was something of considerable news value. Today the problem is the increasing number of old and very old people who need care, to a greater or lesser degree.

The authors have started with the simplest of health care provision, and have given full attention to such experiments as the barefoot doctors in certain developing countries, the local Health Clinics of India and Africa and the simple Medical Centres often established by missionary doctors dealing with huge areas of undeveloped country. This book also deals with design for large and complex hospitals such as for example, the 1000 bed air-conditioned hospital at Baghdad and the newly constructed health complex at Mc Master University, Hamilton, Ontario.

The role of medical care in the pattern of developing and developed countries is increasing. The role of the architect in producing buildings for Health Care which will be efficient, economical and pleasant places, is one which will remain important in the future.

As with the other books in this series, this volume is not intended to deal with the detailed planning problems of health care buildings but is intended to cover the broad strategy and philosophy of such buildings. Those seeking detailed information, dimensions and basic data for the design of buildings will find such material in the appropriate volume of *Planning (9th Edition)*, which will also give further references where this is necessary. It is intended that the two Series of books should be used in parallel and thus form a valuable reference library for those involved with the design and use of buildings of all kinds.

Preface

The advances in medical knowledge and skill that have taken place, together with the parallel revolution in communications that is bringing these advances within the awareness of a constantly increasing number of people throughout the world, have combined in a process which seems irreversible. The provision of health care is a developing facility and its continuous expansion in one form or another to a widening range of the population seems inevitable. The potential cost of this process is vast, as has already been discovered by some countries where the provision of health care has reached its most sophisticated forms.

Buildings that provide for health care fulfil many different functions and accommodate the whole life span of man. They shelter services for the promotion of health and the prevention of illness, for the assistance of natural functions such as childbirth, for the cure of disabilities and the support of those who in a variety of ways are afflicted or incapacitated. These buildings may be said to fall into a number of generic types, but although medicine is largely international the manner in which it is applied in different countries and the forms of building which are appropriate to house it are likely to exhibit differences. Although sharing similarities the buildings will reflect the nature of the organisation and culture, economy and geography of the places in which they are situated.

There are no simple, universal solutions to buildings that provide for health care. Every country presents a different problem and produces different answers – from the highly automated hospital to the itinerant 'barefoot doctor' who needs no premises. Although it is dangerous to generalise it is probably reasonable to say that a broad distinction can be made between the developed and the developing world and that to apply to the latter the solutions of the former without understanding their fundamental dissimilarities is to head for disaster. Not only are there often great differences in belief, social attitudes and infrastructure but the diseases to be mastered are different, as are the problems of climate and communications and the available manpower for staffing. Above all the financial resources that can be raised to initiate and to keep health facilities in action are always limited.

Health care is more positive than the treatment of sick people. Ways of providing places where the sick can be looked after occupy most of this book, but real health care relies on a variety of other things that, although less productive of impressive buildings such as hospitals, are more fundamental. The most basic are the preventive and public health measures that may avoid the necessity of admitting a patient to hospital. The hospital should be the last resort – not the first line of defence – for it is the most elaborate and costly way of combating sickness. If the hospital is not to be overwhelmed, beyond it must lie a network of other interrelated defences and outposts.

It has been well said that the first task of a health service is to reach all the people all the time at the best level of care a country can afford. Buildings are not the main source of health care, for although shelter of various degrees of sophistication is generally necessary and the form of shelter can either help or hinder the tasks performed within, it is the care itself that counts. This depends on people – doctors and surgeons, nurses and auxiliaries, chemists, cooks and social workers, technicians and administrators, and on an organised hierarchy of establishments within which they can work in an interrelated manner. All these must be supported by finance and supplies and backed by a system of education and training that is adequate to provide continuous reinforcements to their numbers.

This book is primarily about the design of buildings in the context of societies in which health care is deliberately organised, whether by state control, insurance arrangements or voluntary effort, or by some combination of these approaches. We have taken a look at both the developed and the developing world and have examined the principal types of building desirable at each level of care in relation to the whole system within which they operate. They range from the services available at the grass roots nearest people's homes, through local clinics and health centres to the small hospital, the general hospital, the teaching hospital and the special services for mental illness and mental handicap. The relation of each facility to others and their place in their social context is explained.

The function that a facility performs is outlined, together with the type of activity it houses and the physical arrangements that in principle can facilitate these activities. The book is an elementary introduction to the subject of health care and does not presume to cover the whole field or to deal with detail. It is in no way intended as a desk-side and/or drawing board reference. We feel that we will have fulfilled our purpose if the book gives the reader the outline of a background against which more detailed publications of guidance and opinion, of which there are many and which often express very divergent views, can be seen in perspective.

There is probably more detailed literature with a bearing on buildings for the health services than on any other category of architecture and much of it is to be found in publications rarely seen by the average architect. Health services are staffed by articulate and dedicated professionals with strong views and, on some things, little consensus of opinion. Thus to write about the design of buildings for health is to walk through a minefield; there is not only the danger of treading directly on explosive material but also the risk of setting off detonations in surrounding areas. Readers are warned that they should not seek any easy answers in this book and that many of its generalisations are all too open to challenge.

A book of this nature necessarily relies on the work, thought and experience of many people and on their writings, or if they are architects more often on their designs. It is impossible to acknowledge them all and if we have misinterpreted some of them it is our own fault. Only a few of the general publications that are reasonably easily available and which seem most relevant have been included in the bibliography, and these are by no means all 'architectural'.

In addition to the architects and others who have supplied plans and photographs and the organisations that have given permission for reproduction and those who have also given valuable guidance, we acknowledge with gratitude the help of people who have read parts of the text or have volunteered information. Their advice has not always been followed in the way they might have wished and none of them bears any responsibility for the result, but we could not have done without them. We are particularly grateful to Frances Aitken, of the Maudsley Hospital, and Gerald White, health planner with Architects' Co-Partnership, for criticisms that have humbled us and suggestions that have helped us to see daylight, and to the staff of the Kings Fund Library whose anonymous assistance has been unfailing.

Anthony Cox
Philip Groves

vii

Contents

Chapter 1
The organisation of health care

Health care presents a different problem in every country, for the way it is organised is a response to geography, climate, historical development, economic situation and social, cultural and political conditions. In the 'advanced' or developed world there is an established and inherited machinery for medical support and a substantial proportion of national resources is devoted to health care.

The various ways in which this is done range from systems of predominantly private enterprise at one extreme to complete State provision at the other, with a variety of combinations in between. In the developing countries, on the other hand, there is usually little inherited machinery of a comparable scale and the provision of health care has to be built up on almost entirely fresh foundations. Appreciation of these differences is fundamental to an understanding of the situation which prevails in a country.

The developed and the developing world

In the USA there are voluntary hospitals and other establishments owned by philanthropic organisations both religious and secular, including many belonging to sickness insurance funds. There are also private establishments run on a commercial basis, and municipal, State and Federal establishments for those unable to afford other forms of care.

Co-ordination is by mutual agreement between the various establishments and the maintenance of technical and medical standards is exercised by independent professional associations. This is not unlike the arrangements that prevailed in the UK prior to 1939.

In central and southern Europe the pattern is dominated by the social insurance institutions and there is a sharp division between the preventive and curative services.

At the other extreme, in the Socialist countries of Eastern Europe there are no private hospitals. All hospitals are part of the public service for preventive and curative health; they enjoy no autonomy and are virtually State controlled from the centre.

In the UK there are private hospitals, some of them commercial and many run by insurance organisations, and there are opportunities for private health care from independent professionals. But since 1948 the National Health Service has established a comprehensive system of inter-related social and medical services that, apart from some minor charges, are available to everyone without fee, irrespective of their age, sex, religion, economic position or ailment.

These services are administered by the local municipal authorities and the hospital authorities, who enjoy a degree of autonomy within budgets, guidelines and legislation established by central government. About 90% of the cost of this National Health Service is met by taxation and the remainder by compulsory insurance contributions from all employers and employees, and by various minor charges.

In the developing areas of the world, where there are greater problems and usually slighter resources, the deliberate organisation of health care is expanding rapidly. It follows almost inevitably from economic and social progress, from the expectations generated by education and from the political pressures of the population. Indeed, it can be said that continuing progress can scarcely take place without it.

Governments are impelled to frame a policy for health care and to assume either an executive or advisory role in implementing it. The pattern is increasingly one of provision by the state, with varying degrees of control, frequently working alongside existing private or philanthropic institutions such as missionary organisations or relatively small commercial units patronised by patients who can afford them. The extent and sophistication of the service depends not only on the country's attitude to social welfare and its administrative structure, but more fundamentally on the level of its economic development – on what it can afford to spend.

Primary, secondary and tertiary care

Whatever their administrative organisation and however they are financed, all systems of health care delivery comprise a range of institutions which, at least in theory, are graded according to their degree of sophistication and specialisation and the level of care that they can provide.

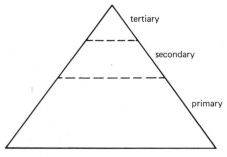

The Health Pyramid

Three main levels can be identified and are usually termed primary, secondary and tertiary. Primary care embraces all the general health practice services, educational, preventive and curative, that are offered to the population at the point of entry into the system. Secondary care comprises the care provided by more specialised services to which people are referred by the primary care services. Tertiary care includes highly specialised services not normally found at secondary level, including super-specialities such as plastic surgery, neurosurgery and heart surgery.

These are very broad divisions, within which there will be finer gradations depending on the appropriate methods of organisation in a particular country, but as basic categorisations they are recognised and understood throughout the world.

The principle of referral of patients from a lower level of care to a higher level as a method of sorting them according to their need for specialist diagnosis or the nature or degree of their disabilities is also universally recognised. Less widely recognised perhaps, or at least less widely practiced, is a referral system that aims to work in both directions, from lower to higher in the first instance and then in reverse, for example during convalescence.

Primary care

At the primary care level are all those health services which are based in the community and relatively accessible to patients and their families; they are at the periphery of the system. These services include preventative health measures such as immunisation programmes, antenatal and child care, and simple diagnosis and treatment. They are operated by doctors, nurses, medical auxiliaries and social workers based in aid posts, dispensaries, clinics and health centres that serve relatively small numbers of people and are situated as close as possible to their homes. This enables medical and other staff to be in contact with their patients' habitual environment.

In the more developed and urbanised countries much of this primary care is provided by the general medical practitioner, who deals with patients at a personal level. Often this doctor works with colleagues in a group practice which shares the services of at least a trained nurse and a secretary. However, in rural areas of the less developed regions of the world the simplest establishment for primary care may be an aid post manned or visited by one auxiliary worker.

Secondary care

At the secondary level is the general hospital, to which patients from a wide surrounding area or district are referred when necessary by primary care units for more sophisticated diagnosis or treatment. Hospitals are an indispensable part of the provision that is made for health because there will always be a proportion of patients who need the particular skills and equipment that can be concentrated in them and because they are essential centres for medical and health education and research.

However, hospitals are inevitably a very expensive element in any health service, for they are costly to build and equip and the money necessary to staff and run them can be enormous. Indeed, their annual running costs may be as much as about a third of the initial capital cost of constructing and equipping them. The running costs of a hospital are particularly high if it needs to accept a large number of in-patients instead of treating them as out-patients. If the in-patients have to stay for a long time then the hospital's expenses are increased and its potential effectiveness reduced. Even in economically advanced countries there are newly constructed hospitals which cannot be brought fully or even partly into use because the funds to maintain them in action cannot be assured.

Apart from any other considerations, such as the pattern of population and the stage that a country has reached in its economic development, it must therefore clearly be the aim of health care to avoid the necessity of referring patients to a general hospital if this is medically practicable. When referral to hospital is essential it is desirable that patients should, if possible, receive their specialist diagnosis and treatment as out-patients and be admitted as in-patients only when that degree of care is essential for their recovery. Even in these cases, patients should not be kept in hospital for longer than is absolutely necessary. If these aims are to be achieved it is vital that there should be primary health care and support outside in the community.

No country can afford to concentrate disproportionately on secondary care. In any event the general hospital will, for most people, be a considerable distance from their homes and will present an alien environment. It is also unlikely to be a suitable centre for primary care even for the minority for whom it is within easy reach.

Community hospitals
At the level of hospital care there has, in the opinion of many people, been an unfortunate tendency in some of the developed countries to concentrate large and sophisticated hospitals of between 300 and 1000 or more beds at regional or district centres. This has often meant the neglect of small local units more acceptable to and more easily within reach of the community. This tendency can also be seen in some parts of the developing world. In addition to the relative simplicity of organising large units in urban areas, the prestige of the big establishment seems sometimes to have taken precedence over the fundamental provision of health care that can be available to the more dispersed elements of population. Even in the UK – a relatively close knit and urbanised community with good communications – there is some feeling that this tendency is undesirable. For instance, there has been little provision of facilities somewhere between the immediately local and primary level of the general medical practitioner in the consulting room or health centre and the often rather remote District General Hospital.

There have been arguments in favour of the concept of the smaller Community Hospital, with perhaps fifty beds and an emphasis on out-patient treatment and Day Care, which is closely in touch with local practitioners and health and social workers. A similar function was often performed in the UK before the advent of the National Health Service by the voluntary 'Cottage hospital', as it used to be called, where patients were attended by their own general practitioners. This is a function that is better regarded as an extension of primary care rather than as a lower level of secondary care. Rural hospitals in many of the African countries and in India play a similar role.

With primary care at the local level and secondary care at district level, tertiary care is at regional level in the more highly specialised hospital. This is usually larger than the general hospital and has a greater emphasis on teaching, particularly of doctors. In most cases there is a close relationship with a medical school and with medical research.

A typical pattern of health care
Although for a variety of reasons it is by no means simple and tidy as this, the pattern of organised health care at primary and secondary levels in a country such as the UK might theoretically take the following shape in outline. (It should be remembered that the UK has a comprehensive health service and a well-established tradition of local general medical practitioners). At the primary level we should find the family doctor having, at the most, some 2300 patients on his list (the present average), many of whom he might of course see rarely if at all.

Family doctors, together with dentists, social workers and other health workers would be grouped in health centres or clinics to serve a population of some 15000, although less in some rural situations and more in the denser urban areas. Some health centres would be linked with a community hospital which might serve a population of the order of 50000. In these hospitals general medical practitioners could oversee the treatment of those of their patients who need more care than they can receive at home but do not need a higher level of hospitalisation.

At the secondary level, we should find the District General Hospital, with a catchment area of up to about 500000 people. Although 'general' in name this might well include certain specialities not provided by other district general hospitals in the larger region.

Health care in developing countries

Whilst it may be generally agreed that the desirable theoretical basis for the promotion of health care is the primary, secondary and tertiary system, it is a pattern more easily described than achieved in practice. It implies a hierarchy of increasingly specialised establishments in which there are very many primary units, immediately available to the individual and the family, and relatively few tertiary units which are more remote.

It is the primary level, the foundation of the pyramid, that probably presents the greatest difficulties. Even in the economically advanced, geographically tight knit and demographically relatively stable communities of the UK the primary level is difficult enough to achieve; it is very much more difficult in some of the larger territories of the developing world. In most of these countries economic resources are slight, the population more dispersed, distances are a more formidable obstacle for want of adequate roads and lack of transport, or because of cultural resistance to travelling outside home ground. The relatively few towns with their greater facilities and varied opportunities act as formidable magnets to attract and retain the better educated medical and technical personnel.

Although many developing countries have embarked on programmes of nationally organised health care delivery, the problems of decentralisation of establishments and their administration are such that for many of the rural population the facilities remain out of reach. In some places there has been a tendency to develop relatively sophisticated hospital services at the centre with the intention of expanding the services outwards and downwards, but all too often this intention remains unfulfilled.

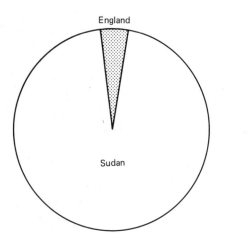

The relative areas of England (population 45.8 million) and the Sudan (population 19.5 million). In 1978 there were 731 Health Centres in England. Under the 1978/84 National Health Programme for the Sudan 1247 Primary Health Care Units need to be built during the seven year period

It would be misleading to generalise about the less developed countries of the world, for they have different characteristics and the degree of their development varies. But some measure of the problem of health service delivery can perhaps be appreciated if it is realised that in many regions about three-quarters of the population is scattered in rural areas and that, in spite of migration to the urban centres, the number is likely to rise. Many rural districts are widely dispersed, are isolated and difficult to reach.

Material resources for dealing with the problem are generally minimal. In some Asian and African countries, for example, it was estimated in the early 1970s that the average per capita income was rather less than one-fortieth of that in France and about one-fiftieth of that in the USA. It has been said that if growth stopped in the USA and the growth of Bangladesh doubled annually it would take 200 years for Bangladesh to overtake the wealth of the USA. In this context much of what the west understands by modern health facilities is largely irrelevant for the majority of the people.

The problems of designing buildings to accommodate the basic facilities are not very complicated. They do, however, demand a degree of understanding which is not always appreciated. They will not be solved by the export of sophisticated systems and equipment from the advanced countries, for these can at the best reach only a tiny minority of the population and may present staffing and maintenance obstacles which are insurmountable.

The difference in the scale of the problem between a developed and a developing country can perhaps be expressed diagrammatically, by comparing the areas of England and the Sudan, and the number of health centres listed for England in the 1979 Hospitals' Year Book with the number of very much simpler, but nevertheless analogous, primary health care units that it is aimed to provide in the Sudan under its present five year plan.

The Sudan has placed a high priority on primary health care delivery and has currently in hand an ambitiously comprehensive programme. Even so, this crude comparison dramatises the differences of population density and distance and demonstrates the irrelevance of applying western criteria to the problem which some of the less developed countries are trying to tackle. This is particularly so if it is appreciated that England possesses a tightly knit network of communications whereas the Sudan has only a few hundred miles of metalled road and in large areas of the country much of the population is nomadic.

Although the Sudan with its huge expanses of desert is not a typical country, either in size, nature or distribution of population, it should not be thought that other developing countries do not have similar difficulties. Frequently the executive strains of their civil authorities – regional, provincial and local – inhibit the decentralisation of the administration of health services and their correlation with other social services such as public health.

Most developing countries have problems arising from distance and lack of transport and telecommunications. They have widely dispersed settlements and relatively few urban centres, poor housing, lack of clean water or adequate drainage, or suitable building materials and labour in the places where they are most needed. Perhaps above all, they have problems of finance and appropriate medical and paramedical staffing, of health education, medical supplies and contact between staff and the patients' homes.

A working party of the Medical Committee of the Conference of Missionary Societies observed in 1975 that in reasonably open and reasonably flat country a high proportion of the population would travel 4.8 km (3 miles) to a health centre but that beyond five miles attendance was sporadic. They concluded that in these circumstances a centre was theoretically required at the middle of every 259 sq km (100 sq miles) of territory. They also noted that a bullock cart can travel for six hours at 3 m.p.h. without halt and that this is a reasonable practicable time between emergency referral at a health centre and reception at a hospital.

It followed, again theoretically, that if the centre was more than about 32 km (20 miles) from the hospital some other form of transport would be needed. These simple figures drive home the realities of the situation in many parts of the world, for the close network of services that might ideally follow from them will clearly be unattainable for a long time.

Grass roots care

National planning, organisation and finance are fundamental to any system of health delivery which can hope to reach all the people, but there is good reason to think that in much of the developing world the most effective results are obtained by building upwards from the grass roots with the involvement of the local community rather than by extending the existing and more sophisticated facilities in the urban centres outwards to the villages.

With the use of relatively simple medical techniques and personnel and accommodation appropriate and acceptable to the community priorities are more likely to be in the right order and the primary problems of health education, elementary hygiene, sanitation and nutrition can be tackled at the point where they really matter, and can be seen to matter, and where the improved results from simple medical care can help to breed confidence in the efficacy of new methods.

China probably provides the most vivid example of this approach to basic health care. A policy aimed at the prevention of disease and the enlistment of the population in mass health and sanitation campaigns produced remarkable results. Locally recruited rural youths, 'barefoot doctors' with three months' formal training (of whom in the mid 1970s there were said to be over a million) acted as educators, practiced preventative medicine, and treated minor illnesses. There were analogous worker doctors in the factories and the cities.

Of all countries China presents the clearest picture in recognising the impossibility of developing 'normal' traditional health services based on a doctor-patient relationship if the needs of a large rural population spread over a vast territory are to be met, and of the value of the participation of the community itself in tackling the problem.

Other countries provide examples of nationally organised but simplified methods of health care delivery, each different because the method employed responds to different circumstances, but all sharing the characteristics of the grass roots approach. In Tanzania, where a start was made on regrouping the widely scattered population into economically viable communities of between a 100 and 500 families that could be provided with basic amenities, similar emphasis was placed since 1973 on local self-reliance and disease prevention. It was intended that each community should construct its own health post, staffed by its own medical aid whom it chosed and supported.

In 1977 there were 5500 such communities with health posts, and in addition rural dispensaries on a scale of one for 6000–8000 people which provided higher level diagnosis, treatment, and maternal and child-health services. These were backed up by sixty nine health centres, one hundred and twenty eight hospitals, and by mobile teams taking health care out to areas of thin coverage.

In the Republic of Niger much reliance has been up to now placed on volunteers for looking after primary health needs in remote areas. The Republic paid for their training and refresher courses, their medical supplies and petrol, but the local village health workers, who were capable of giving basic treatment and teaching hygiene and the improvement of nutrition, were unpaid. Starting in 1963, by 1974 there were nearly 800 volunteer health workers and over 450 village midwives. Many rural dispensaries had been upgraded to health centres.

In 1962 Venezuela introduced a 'simplified medicine' scheme in order to reach its dispersed rural population. It was based on a network of village dispensaries, each serving from 500 to several thousand people. These were manned by trained auxiliary health workers who were supervised and supported by rural health posts providing care for a semi-rural population and staffed by a doctor and auxiliaries. These in turn were backed up by health centres with basic hospital facilities, and finally by specialised referral hospitals. The training of auxiliaries took four months, followed by in-service training.

Financed by government, the local communities were nevertheless encouraged to participate in running costs and to contribute in kind towards construction and equipment. Although progress was fairly slow, by the end of the first eleven years over three hundred dispensaries and nearly five hundred health posts were serving about 280 000 people, some 12% of the rural population.

In the Sudan the primary health care programme

introduced in 1975 aims to make primary care of a socially and culturally acceptable nature as accessible as possible to the whole population. It aims to provide a community-orientated service and foster community development rather than being directed mainly towards individuals. Emphasis is placed on local participation in organisation and the supply of materials and equipment, and on voluntary labour for construction and for transporting the sick.

In the settled areas, a network of primary health care units is envisaged, each based on a population of some four thousand within a radius of attendance of about ten miles. It is proposed that five of these units should be supported by a dispensary for the purpose of referral and the supply of drugs, each complex so formed serving a population of about 24 000 and being integrated through a referral system with Health Centres and secondary establishments. It is the intention that by 1984 there should be at least one community health worker for every four thousand people in the settled areas, and one nomadic worker (selected from amongst themselves by the nomad community) for every 1500 nomads.

Health care in the UK

By contrast, it may be of value to outline the organisational structure of health care in Britain, an area smaller than these countries but one that developed earlier, with a population very much larger (with the exception of course of China). In the UK there is a concentrated inheritance of diverse medical and technical skills, of plant and of buildings, and of a complex web of social services related to health care.

The national per capita expenditure on health, great though it is, cannot be said to match some other developed countries, for in relation to its population and its national income Britain's expenditure in the mid 1970s was about half that of Sweden, somewhat less than half that of the USA, and also less than that of France, Finland, the Netherlands, Norway and West Germany, and, further afield, of Australia and Canada. Nevertheless it is a national service that has brought health care within the reach of everyone, employing in all just over one doctor per thousand head of population and well over a third of a million hospital nursing staff in addition to the many others engaged in auxiliary duties or in various forms of work in the community.

The British structure is not described here as a model applicable to all situations, but as an indication of an attempt to provide health care at all levels for the whole population as a single unified service in which the nationalised health authorities and the local government organisations play complementary roles. It must be appreciated that in the UK the greater part of the population is in the towns, whereas in developing countries the greater part is in the rural areas and is often encouraged by their government to stay there. Any structure must be seen in that light.

Since 1912 there had been a National Health Insurance Scheme which entitled patients to free treatment by a general practitioner and to free medicine, but these benefits were limited to wage earners with relatively low incomes. Those people above this level and the self-employed, wives who did not go out to work, and children, did not qualify. These had either to pay medical fees (or apply for public assistance if they could not afford them) or they might attend the casualty department of a voluntary charitable hospital. Anyone admitted to hospital, whether insured or not, usually had to pay what the hospital considered appropriate.

It was a fundamental principle from the beginning of the National Health Service in 1948, and it remains so still, that it should be available to all people, should cover all necessary forms of health care, and should be provided free of charge to the patient at the time of use. (This is in contrast to some other Western European countries where patients pay a proportion of the charge when they avail themselves of the service). Costs were to be met from taxation and compulsory insurance contributions by employers and employees.

When the National Health Service was introduced most general practitioners became 'independent contractors' to the service and most voluntary hospitals, including teaching hospitals and the hospitals previously run by the local authorities, were transferred to national ownership. Fundamentally it was a rationalisation of already highly but arbitrarily developed health care delivery services to make them available to all in accordance with medical need and by no other criteria.

As the Royal Commission on the service pointed out in 1979, one of the most significant achievements was to free people from the fear of being unable to afford treatment for acute or chronic illness. That patients often waited too long for treatment had to be seen in the light of disappointingly slow national economic growth and the mounting costs which were in no small part a consequence of developments in medical, nursing and therapeutic techniques to levels of sophistication and expense that were not originally foreseen.

It may be added that as any health service develops so do people's expectations and demands increase: it has been said of the USA that if the demand for health care was to be fully met, the entire national budget would need to be devoted to this one social service.

At its inception the service was organised in three separate parts – the family practitioner services, the hospital and specialist services, and those health services which were provided by the local authorities. Because it was based on existing establishments, each of these three parts was organised within different geographical boundaries and was separately planned and financed. Because of the interdependence of the three parts the service was reorganised in the mid 1970s to improve their co-ordination and to bring them together under a single authority.

The elements of health care brought together comprised the hospitals and specialised services (at the secondary and tertiary levels), the family practitioner services and school health service, and the personal health services which together with environmental health (housing, sanitation, refuse disposal, etc) are the responsibility of local government. The personal health services include health centres, health visiting, home nursing and midwifery, maternity and child health care, family planning, medical and nursing arrangements for the prevention of illness, vaccination, immunisation and epidemiological work, and all the ambulance services.

At the present time the service is organised on three administrative levels: central, regional and area. Some areas are subdivided into districts. The central government Department of Health and Social Security is responsible to Parliament for the health services as a whole. This government department determines national policy, carries out the central strategic planning and monitors the operational results. It settles the nature and scale of the services provided throughout the country, allocates resources to regions, and carries out some types of research and purchasing.

Apart from the costs of central administration and various minor items the allocation of finance is divided into three main sections. About 15% goes to the personal social services through Local Authorities, 15% to the fees of family practitioners, dentists, opticians and retail pharmacists, and 65% or more to the Health Authorities for the capital and revenue costs of hospital and community health facilities, apportioned between the regions. Some 60% of the total expenditure is devoted to children, the old, the disabled and the mentally ill and handicapped.

Below the central department there are fourteen Regional Health Authorities in England alone. Their boundaries do not necessarily coincide with county or other local government boundaries and the areas they cover differ considerably in extent, being related to density of population rather than to geographical size. Each is responsible for the planning and the general supervision of operations within its region.

The authority identifies the services needing a regional rather than an area approach, co-ordinates the plans of its various areas, allocates their resources and monitors performance. It co-ordinates regional services including ambulance and blood transfusion services. It is responsible for the design and construction of new buildings but may delegate some of this to areas.

Within these fourteen regions there are ninety Area Health Authorities. There are at least three Authorities in each region and considerably more in regions containing the larger conurbations. The areas share the same boundaries with local government authorities, an important factor for the co-ordination of services. Each Area Authority is responsible for planning and operational control within its domain, co-ordinated with the complimentary health services of the local authorities. It plans the services in consultation with these local authorities and the Regional Health Authority. Amongst the responsibilities of the areas are the planning and development of health centres, the administration of contracts with medical and dental practitioners, opticians and pharmacists, and the arrangements for nurses and other aides to work with family doctors.

Some areas contain substantial medical and dental teaching facilities, notably those associated with universities. These are known as Teaching Areas and are administered as part of the regions in which they are situated.

Most Area Health Authorities are broken down into Health Districts. Outside London there are one hundred and fifty-four Districts, varying in number between one and five per area. The District boundaries do not necessarily coincide with those of Local Government. A District usually serves a population of between 200 000 and 500 000 and it is on the District that the day-to-day running of services is based.

In a consultative paper, *Patients First,* published at the end of 1979, the Government announced its intention of simplifying the structure in England. The aim was to encourage as many management decisions as possible to be taken at a local level, in the hospital and the community, with the minimum of interference from central authorities.

There had been widespread criticism that the re-organisation of the mid-1970's had resulted in too many tiers and too many administrators, resulting in a top heavy bureaucracy unable to take decisions quickly. It was proposed to eliminate the Area tier altogether and to establish district health authorities with a much greater degree of autonomy; the regions would co-ordinate strategic plans and allocate resources but would stand back from the operational activities of the districts.

Regional Health Authorities were to make proposals for the restructuring of their areas and once these were agreed by Government were to proceed to put the changes into effect. Many of the changes were expected to be accomplished by the middle of 1982, with the aim of completing the process by the end of 1983.

Some of the present areas may become district health authorities, some of the present districts may be unchanged and others be subject to boundary alterations. The intention is that, ideally, the new district authorities should be responsible for a locality which is 'natural' in terms of social geography and health care and large enough to justify the range of specialities normally provided by a district general hospital. Its boundaries would coincide with those of the other authorities responsible for social services, housing and education. In the main the districts would have populations of between 200 000 and 500 000.

Before the reorganisation of the National Health Service in the 1970s and the emphasis on increased community care, three acute beds per thousand population was the normal standard for a District General Hospital. This has now been reduced to two per thousand (plus a complement of maternity, geriatric and psychiatric beds). Thus in current circumstances a District General Hospital, if it is the sole provision in its district, might typically consist of between about 400 and 1000 beds.

Altogether there are about 2750 National Health Service hospitals, providing a total of some 480 000 beds in addition to outpatient and accident and emergency services. They range from the large psychiatric hospital with over 1500 beds to the local 'cottage' hospital with 50 beds or less. Some hospitals provide a few 'pay beds', which offer a degree of additional privacy and the opportunity of supervision by a consultant of the patient's choice, on the basis of a fee. The number of pay beds has been falling steadily; in 1979 there were just under 3000.

In addition to the National Health Service hospitals there are a significant number of independent establishments which provide health care. Finance for private patients can be provided through medical insurance schemes entirely separate from government provisions. Rather than offering comprehensive care or emergency services, the independent hospitals usually cater for specific categories of patients, such as maternity, psychiatric, the elderly, the chronic, and the convalescent. In the field of surgery independent hospitals concentrate on 'cold surgery', which can be arranged well in advance. In 1977 there were 1249 registered private hospitals and nursing homes, providing some 34 550 beds, about 6.7% of the total number of beds in Britain. They are mostly relatively small establishments of well under a hundred beds.

Chapter 2
Community health services

The previous chapter emphasised the differences in the scale and nature of health care in the developed and the less developed world. Attention was given to the impracticability, unless it was supported by an infrastructure of primary care, of relying upon the large hospital, which besides being extremely costly to run is necessarily relatively remote, even in an urbanised society, and can have few firm roots in the community.

Primary care in the community

This chapter deals with some examples of units designed for primary care in the community, to which people can have easy access. Whilst they can play a positive role in guidance and the encouragement of health as distinct from dealing with sickness, for most people such units are likely to be their first point of contact with a health service, where they can be treated so that reference to a more specialised establishment is unnecessary. In the UK these are principally the 'surgeries' of the general medical practitioners; they are sometimes grouped together with accommodation for some of the social and public health services and are known as health centres. Associated with the health centre there may be a few beds to provide a small local or community hospital, although this development remains relatively rare.

By contrast, in the less developed areas of the world medical practitioners are generally few and far between and are frequently beyond the pockets of the majority of people. Communities are very much more widely dispersed. Thus the facilities for primary care, although aiming to fulfil a similar function and sometimes known as health centres, are usually of a simpler nature.

Health centres as places for primary care may be purely preventive or purely curative, or may integrate both these aspects. Integrated health centres where organised preventive services were combined with the primary care of general medical practitioners first appeared in the USSR as part of national policy in the 1920s, when a network of such establishments began to be set up as elements in a regional framework, with polyclinics and hospitals at secondary level.

However, despite the recognition in the British Ministry of Health's Dawson report of 1920 that 'preventive and curative medicine cannot be separated on any sound principle' it was not until 1945 that the concept of organised community care based on the integrated health centre began to gain wide acceptance in the UK, or indeed in most other countries.

The term health centre can signify different things. Regrettably it is generally used to designate something that might more accurately be described as a centre reluctantly visited by people with minor sickness in the hope that they can be restored to health without having to go to hospital. A unit that demonstrated a different and more positive approach, better fitted to its title, was an independent British project that first attracted some notice nearly fifty years ago. It is of interest both for the idea behind it and for the physical form into which the idea was translated.

The Pioneer Health Centre at Peckham in South London was a voluntary experiment, independent of government and the local authority. It began in a small way in 1926 and was finally established, much expanded, in purpose-built premises in 1935. Intended as a centre for the local community, where the emphasis was on the promotion and the monitoring of health, local families were invited to use it as a club and as a condition of membership were offered periodic health overhaul of the whole family. It also provided ancillary services for infants, children and adults.

The function of the Pioneer Health Centre was primarily preventive and did not extend to treatment, and its nature was deliberately that of a community

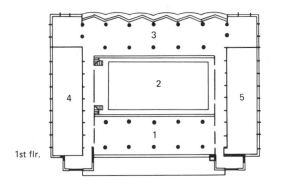
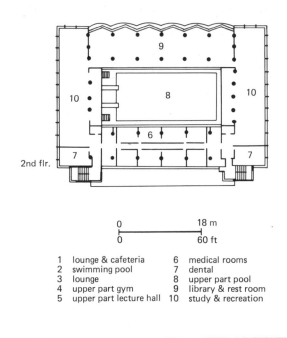

1st flr.

2nd flr.

The core of the Pioneer Health Centre at Peckham was the swimming pool, visible through glazed screens from the social rooms flanking it. The Centre was a family club, providing the opportunity for the observation and monitoring of health; throughout the building a sense of community and flexibility of movement was encouraged by open planning and visibility from one area to another. Designer: Sir Owen Williams

0   18 m
0   60 ft

1	lounge & cafeteria	6	medical rooms
2	swimming pool	7	dental
3	lounge	8	upper part pool
4	upper part gym	9	library & rest room
5	upper part lecture hall	10	study & recreation

The Pioneer Health Centre. A day nursery and open-air play space, a gymnasium, lecture theatre and workshops were at ground level. The pool was on the floor above, flanked by lounges and cafeteria. (Photo: Pioneer Health Centre Ltd)

centre. Intended for the leisure use of 2000 families it was planned around an indoor swimming pool and had a day nursery and playground, a gymnasium, lounge, cafeteria, library and lecture room, and a few rooms for medical and dental inspection. It was an individual and isolated experiment and was built at a period before a health service was accessible to everybody, when the fear of going to a doctor and of the possible expense and loss of earnings that sickness might involve was very real. The 1939–45 war interrupted its activities and it continued for only a few years afterwards.

An entirely different type of health centre was built by a local authority in Finsbury, London, at about the same time as the Peckham centre. It is perhaps best known because of the attention it attracted architecturally.

The purpose of the Finsbury Health Centre was to bring together under one roof all the health services for which the local authority was responsible, which had previously been dispersed in different parts of the borough. Thus it housed the offices of the departments of the Medical Officer of Health and the Sanitary Inspector, the public cleansing and disinfecting station and the mortuary. For public use it provided a lecture hall and suites of rooms for clinics and treatment, for chiropody, dentistry, tuberculosis and for electrical treatment. But unlike the later health centres in the UK it made no provision for the general medical practitioner, whose services were not a function of the local authority.

In the UK the term health centre is sometimes used to describe the accommodation that, although specially built for the purpose, houses only a group practice of general practitioners with some ancillary services such as a secretary and a nurse and does not have the

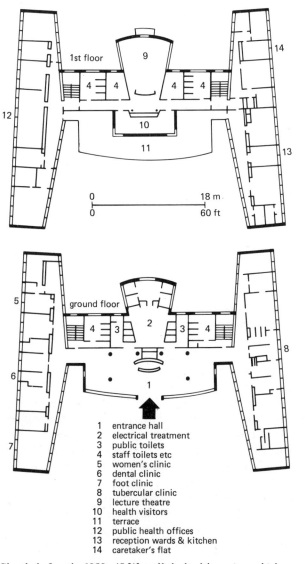

1 entrance hall
2 electrical treatment
3 public toilets
4 staff toilets etc
5 women's clinic
6 dental clinic
7 foot clinic
8 tubercular clinic
9 lecture theatre
10 health visitors
11 terrace
12 public health offices
13 reception wards & kitchen
14 caretaker's flat

Shortly before the 1939–45 War all the health services which were the responsibility of the (borough of Finsbury) and dispersed in different places were brought together in one building. Offices and clinics occupied the two wings. The borough disinfection and cleansing station and the mortuary were below part of the ground floor, entered from the rear. Architects: Tecton

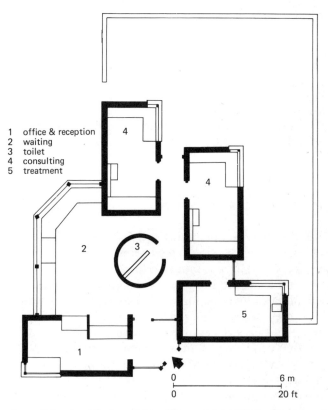

1 office & reception
2 waiting
3 toilet
4 consulting
5 treatment

A small 'surgery' for two doctors. The reception office and waiting area are screened from the entrances to the two consulting rooms and the treatment room, which overlook a walled garden. There is a separate entrance for the doctors. Architects: Aldington and Craig

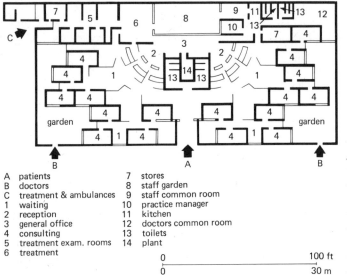

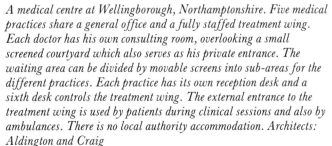

A	patients	7	stores
B	doctors	8	staff garden
C	treatment & ambulances	9	staff common room
1	waiting	10	practice manager
2	reception	11	kitchen
3	general office	12	doctors common room
4	consulting	13	toilets
5	treatment exam. rooms	14	plant
6	treatment		

0   100 ft
0   30 m

A medical centre at Wellingborough, Northamptonshire. Five medical practices share a general office and a fully staffed treatment wing. Each doctor has his own consulting room, overlooking a small screened courtyard which also serves as his private entrance. The waiting area can be divided by movable screens into sub-areas for the different practices. Each practice has its own reception desk and a sixth desk controls the treatment wing. The external entrance to the treatment wing is used by patients during clinical sessions and also by ambulances. There is no local authority accommodation. Architects: Aldington and Craig

close links with the local authority's personal and social health services that are the characteristic feature of the integrated health centre.

Such accommodation is better called a medical centre or by its customary but rather misleading title of 'surgery'. It is little different in function from the converted domestic accommodation used by many private general practitioners, except that it may be designed to fulfil its purpose more conveniently. It does however share with the integrated health centre some fundamental planning principles, albeit in a simple form, particularly in the arrangements that are desirable for the reception of patients and for the relationship between reception desk, waiting spaces, patient's records and consulting and treatment rooms.

Health centres in the UK

With the introduction of the National Health Service in 1948 a network of integrated primary health centres was envisaged. It was intended that they should provide accommodation for rent by groups of general medical practitioners, nurses and administrative staff, where they could be housed together with the staff of the preventive services of the local authority.

At first progress was slow and few were built, probably partly because general practitioners, like dentists, chemists and opticians, were independent 'contractors' to the health service and responsible for the provision of their own premises. They were probably reluctant to participate in a nationally organised scheme, fearing that the proposal might be a first step towards becoming state employees and

preferring to safeguard their independent position. But for largely practical reasons professional partnerships or group practices steadily increased in popularity during this period, and by the mid 1960s it was estimated that only about a quarter of all general practitioners were still running individual private practices.

By this time the Government had become seriously concerned about the escalating cost of hospital care; it was clear that if this was to be checked a much higher priority needed to be given to care in the community itself – in short, as far as possible to make it unnecessary for patients to be treated in hospital. Increased emphasis was placed on the importance of trying to integrate the work of general practitioners with the socially based services provided by local government. Thus although by the end of 1958 only ten new health centres had been completed in England, by 1968 the number had risen to one hundred and ten and has subsequently continued to increase, although partly for financial reasons the pace has not been as rapid as might have been hoped. Between 1972 and 1977 their number rose from 212 to 731 in England and Wales, and a further 200 were planned for the future.

The number of patients a general practitioner has on his list in Britain ranges from about 1000 to 3500. On average, practices using health centres comprise four or five practitioners and a group of this size is likely to serve some 15 000 patients; but the size of health centres varies considerably, depending in part on their location, the extent of their catchment area, the policy of the local authority and the number and size of the local group practices that wish to be accommodated in the building.

Buildings range from a centre for a small practice of two or three doctors with a nurse, secretary and a minimum of local authority accommodation (perhaps an office for Home Help and some space for health education) to three or four practices with in addition dental surgeons, physiotherapists, chiropodists, midwives, district nurses, health visitors, school health services and, increasingly, provision for the education in community health of medical students, student nurses and student health visitors. From a rural catchment area of some 10 000 people or less at one end of the scale, the centre may cater for a population of 30 000 or more in an urban area.

The more comprehensive the centre's facilities the more difficult it is to provide a building that encourages the integration of a variety of personnel, and the more valuable it will be if it can succeed in doing so. It can, of course, do no more than facilitate and encourage integration, for a team approach to community care does not follow automatically from bringing together in the same building different people with different responsibilities, employed by different authorities.

Activities in the health centre

The activities of the health centre are of three distinct types, arranged in sessions which may be daily, weekly or less frequent. Only one of these types of activity is likely to be taking place at any one time. Firstly, there is personal care, when the patient visits a general practitioner, a nurse or another individual worker, normally on his own initiative, to obtain help or treatment for a personal problem or ailment. Secondly, there are clinic sessions attended by numbers of people and organised for a particular purpose, such as antenatal supervision or immunisation. Thirdly, there are group activities conducted in classes, such as antenatal relaxation, keep-fit exercises, talks and demonstrations.

Although these divisions relate to British practice the function of a health centre anywhere in the world is likely to embrace these three principal types of activity.

In the UK the health centre is the general practitioners' base for home care when they are not engaged in 'surgery' sessions. It is also the base for the personal services provided by the local authority in the form of home nurses, health visitors, midwives and social workers. Thus the health centre has the potential to reach out into the community rather than being merely a place to which the community comes for help, and it is also, increasingly, a base for teaching and research. In some communities it will become a social meeting point for mothers with young children, particularly if they attend regular sessions, and for

some young mothers it may provide their easiest opportunity to meet other women in a new community. For these reasons alone a relaxed and pleasant environment is important.

Accommodation

The accommodation falls into five main categories: reception and waiting space; administration and storage of patients' records; rooms for consulting, interview and treatment (some of which, such as dentistry or chiropody, may contain special fixed equipment); space for class activities; and ancillary and communal rooms for use by the staff.

It has been argued that it is regrettable that the integrated health centres in Britain do not also provide a few beds where the general practitioner can have regular access to some of his patients. This would avoid the necessity of having to refer them to the more specialised services of a general hospital, which may not in fact be strictly necessary for the patient or even suitable. Indeed in 1968 the Royal Commission on Medical Education predicted that there would be a case for the provision of short-stay beds and facilities for minor surgery.

The concept of the small Community Hospital is relevant in this context, and there are examples of similarly extended health centres in some other countries.

Internal planning of health centres

Probably the most important factors to be taken into account in the overall plan form of a health centre, whatever its size, are simplicity and clarity in the circulation flow of patients, and the need to avoid this circulation becoming confused with that of the staff. It is also desirable to combine clarity with an atmosphere which is comfortable and human in scale. Some patients will be arriving at the centre for the first time, some will be visiting a doctor for diagnosis, treatment or follow-up, others merely for a renewed prescription or the signature of a certificate. Some may be disabled or infirm, old or confused, or may be in wheelchairs; some will have children or will come with relatives.

The movement of patients may be considerable and as far as is practicable must be separated from the movement of staff and the transfer of records from central storage to consulting rooms. Each doctor may be seeing ten patients an hour, sometimes more, and a group of six doctors may generate a patient flow, in and out, of sixty an hour, or one hundred and twenty journeys in one direction or another. It is important that those journeys should be short and simple and should not conflict with other journeys that staff are

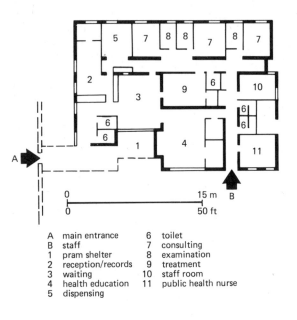

A main entrance
B staff
1 pram shelter
2 reception/records
3 waiting
4 health education
5 dispensing
6 toilet
7 consulting
8 examination
9 treatment
10 staff room
11 public health nurse

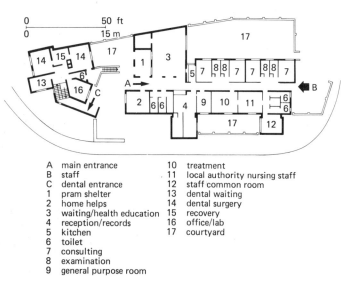

A main entrance
B staff
C dental entrance
1 pram shelter
2 home helps
3 waiting/health education
4 reception/records
5 kitchen
6 toilet
7 consulting
8 examination
9 general purpose room
10 treatment
11 local authority nursing staff
12 staff common room
13 dental waiting
14 dental surgery
15 recovery
16 office/lab
17 courtyard

(left)
A small health centre at Bishops Lydeard, Somerset, with three consulting rooms and separate examination rooms. There is a dispensary, and space for health education and for a local authority nurse. Architect: B. C. Adams, Somerset County Council

(below, left)
A health centre at Glastonbury, Somerset, with a dental unit in a separate building. The four consulting rooms have separate examination rooms; there are combined waiting and health education spaces, and rooms for home helps and local authority nursing staff. All rooms overlook walled courtyards and are screened from the street and the car park behind the building. Boilers, stores and dark room are on a lower floor of the dental unit. Architect: B. C. Adams, Somerset County Council

(below)
The entrance to the Glastonbury health centre. The dental unit is on the left.

making about the building. The patient should arrive at the consulting room in as relaxed a mood as possible.

Flow patterns

The normal pattern of flow of patients generated by general practitioners during a 'surgery' session is arrival at the centre and disposal of car, bicycle or push-chair. Bicycles and particularly push-chairs need covered parking space, which in some communities should be sited so that the reception staff can keep an eye on them. Inside the building the pattern

consists of: reporting at the reception point (which may be occupied with other patients on their way out or collecting prescriptions or making an enquiry); waiting until called (and perhaps ensuring that children are cared for); finding the way to the correct consulting room or group of consulting rooms and perhaps waiting again until the doctor is ready; during consultation perhaps moving to an examination room and after consultation perhaps receiving treatment in a different room; and finally, on the way out, perhaps visiting the reception point again or collecting children.

(right)
A health centre at Portishead, Somerset. A double corridor plan with two ranges of consulting rooms and separate examination rooms. Accommodation includes a dental surgery and rooms for chiropody, speech therapy, a social worker and local authority nurses. A large staff common room and small offices for a nurse and secretary are on an upper floor. Architect: B. C. Adams, Somerset County Council

A	main entrance & pram shelter	10 social worker
B	staff	11 administrator
1	reception/records	12 garden
2	waiting	13 chiropody
3	health education	14 consulting
4	speech therapy	15 examination
5	nurses	16 treatment
6	toilets	17 dental surgery
7	interview	18 recovery
8	rest room	19 dark room
9	typing	20 store

(below, right)
The waiting space and reception counter at South Poplar. (Photo: Henk Snoek/Fabienne de Backer)

(below)
A compact health centre in South Poplar, London, constructed from sixteen modular units surrounding a central toplit waiting area that is screened on one side from the staff rooms and open on the other to the patients' corridor. Architects: Derek Stow and Partners

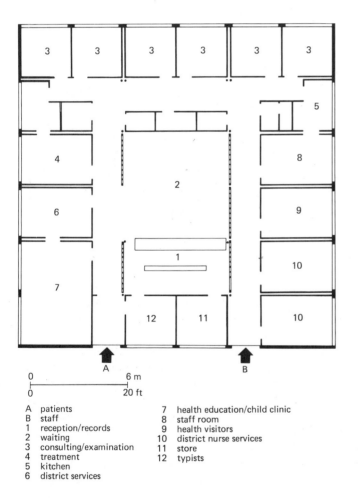

A	patients	7	health education/child clinic
B	staff	8	staff room
1	reception/records	9	health visitors
2	waiting	10	district nurse services
3	consulting/examination	11	store
4	treatment	12	typists
5	kitchen		
6	district services		

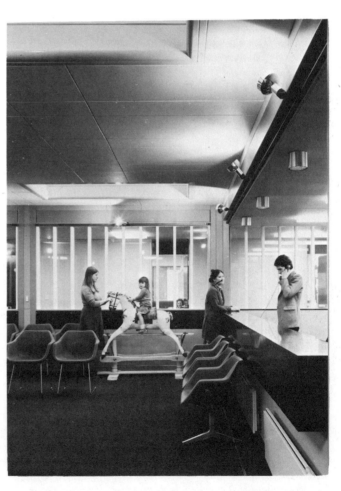

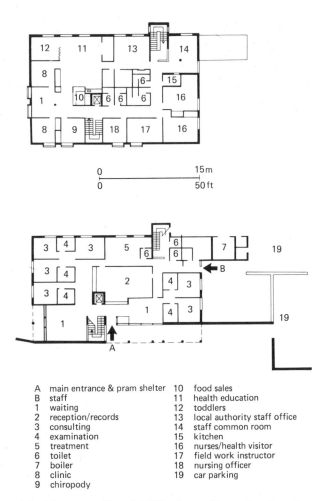

A	main entrance & pram shelter
B	staff
1	waiting
2	reception/records
3	consulting
4	examination
5	treatment
6	toilet
7	boiler
8	clinic
9	chiropody
10	food sales
11	health education
12	toddlers
13	local authority staff office
14	staff common room
15	kitchen
16	nurses/health visitor
17	field work instructor
18	nursing officer
19	car parking

A health centre at Mansfield Woodhouse, Nottinghamshire. Six consulting rooms with separate examination rooms are arranged in two practice groups with separate reception counters and waiting areas. The health education room and local authority services are on the upper floor. Architect: H. T. Swain, Nottinghamshire County Council

Mansfield Woodhouse. The larger of the two waiting spaces, separated from the smaller by the stair and main entrance. (Photo: A. Hurst)

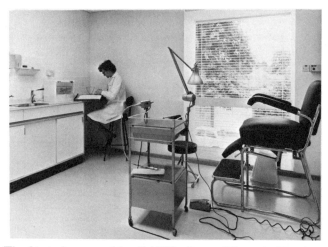

The chiropody room at Mansfield Woodhouse. (Photo: A. Hurst)

There may be other flows of patients, some of them at the same time (e.g. to dentists or chiropodists) but the movement generated by the general practitioners will be by far the largest. It is worth noting that people who are unfamiliar with a building like to leave it by the same route as that by which they entered and that staff, particularly general practitioners, need a way in and out independent of that used by patients.

The reception area

The reception point needs to adjoin the store of patients' records and is sometimes combined with it; rapid retrieval of records is essential, and so is their confidentiality. The reception area should be immediately apparent and welcoming on entering the centre. It should be so arranged in relation to the waiting space that confidential conversations can take place between patient and receptionist, and it may be combined with the distribution point for welfare foods and medicines.

The size and the number of staff in attendance depend on the through-put. There is likely to be fairly busy telephone traffic. If there is an appointment system patients' records can be selected and delivered to the doctors before the session begins, but if not, it is essential to have particularly easy access from records to consulting rooms.

In some of the larger health centres the reception point is more akin to an enquiry counter. There may be separate receptionists and waiting spaces dispersed in the territory of each medical practice or dental suite. This will not eliminate the need for some general waiting space in the main reception area.

A main entrance & pram shelter
B doctors
C disabled
1 waiting
2 sub waiting
3 reception/records
4 food sales & kitchen
5 health education
6 toddlers
7 consulting
8 examination
9 chiropody
10 treatment
11 nurses room
12 store
13 boilers

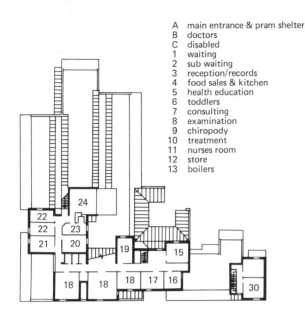

Pershore. The entrance from the street, leading to the covered court. The caretaker's house is on the right, linked to the main building by the dental suite. (Photo: Martin Charles)

14 incinerator
15 director, social services
16 medical officer of health
17 clerk to MOH
18 health visitor
19 group adviser
20 administrator
21 clerks office
22 GP clerical staff
23 staff rest room
24 common room
25 dental waiting
26 dental surgery
27 recovery
28 dark room/lab.
29 telephone eqpt.
30 caretaker's house

N ←

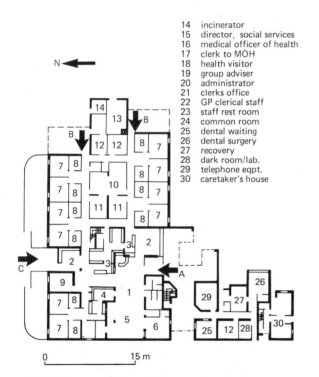

0   15 m

One of the sub-waiting spaces at Pershore, overlooking the covered court. (Photo: Martin Charles)

A health centre at Pershore, Worcestershire, for two group practices. Consulting and examination rooms are arranged along two corridors flanking a central treatment room. There are two reception counters and sub-waiting spaces in addition to a general waiting area adjoining the health education room. The dental suite is entered separately and adjoins a caretaker's house. Accommodation upstairs includes offices for the Area Medical Officer of Health, the social services and health visitors and a common room. The building is near the town centre; the main entrance adjoins a covered court, where prams can be left in full view of the waiting space, and is approached either from the street or by a path across a garden linking it to a public library and a car park. Architects: Darbourne and Darke

The toplit treatment room at Pershore. (Photo: Martin Charles)

It is widely accepted that a large and impersonal waiting space is to be avoided, and that it should provide a sense of seclusion from other traffic. The space needed will depend on whether there is an appointment system, for this obviously reduces it considerably. But even with appointments waiting spaces tend to become overcrowded at times and the division of the space into separate wings or bays can be helpful in reducing the scale, particularly if more than about five consulting rooms are served from it. It is also more peaceful and can help to reduce the risk of cross-infection.

It is important that all the main waiting space should be easily visible from the reception point and that the route from it to the consulting rooms should be easily identifiable, as short as possible, and should not involve crossing busy staff circulation routes such as those between reception, records and the consulting rooms. It is also an advantage for control purposes if the patient's route from main waiting space to consulting rooms can be observed from the reception point. Small subsidiary spaces close to the consulting rooms (not merely chairs in a corridor) where patients can wait briefly immediately before seeing the doctor, can be valuable; they are particularly important if in a large centre the consulting rooms have to be unduly far from the reception point and main waiting area.

Consulting rooms

Opinions differ about the best arrangements for the consulting rooms themselves, and whether separate examination rooms are desirable. Undressing, examination and minor treatment can all be done in the consulting room if it is large enough, but they can also take place in an adjacent examination room. The latter procedure can save some of the doctor's time, give greater flexibility and enable a nurse to deal with a patient in an examination room while the doctor continues with another patient in the consulting room.

However there is much to be said for doing without examination rooms, partly from the patient's point of view and also in the interest of future uses. A series of standard units of consulting room size, suitable for most of the interview, examination, minor treatment or office functions, can offer a more flexible arrangement, particularly if the number of general practitioners or the balance of other staff changes in the future. Sometimes a suite of consulting rooms is provided with intercommunicating doors so that a doctor can, for example, make use of the next room whilst a patient he has finished examining is dressing.

If separate examination rooms are provided they should adjoin the consulting room and should not be on the opposite side of a corridor. There is sometimes a door between consulting and examination rooms,

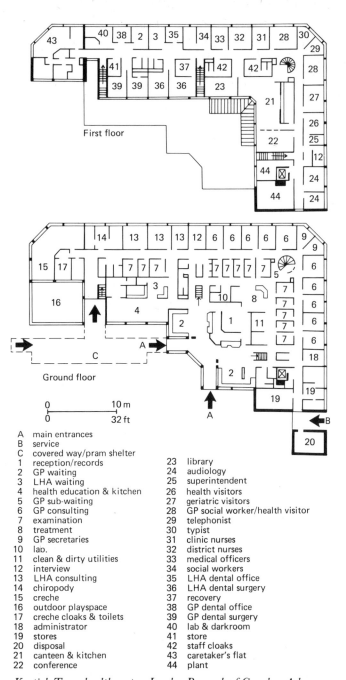

First floor

Ground floor

0		10 m
0		32 ft

A   main entrances
B   service
C   covered way/pram shelter

1	reception/records	23	library
2	GP waiting	24	audiology
3	LHA waiting	25	superintendent
4	health education & kitchen	26	health visitors
5	GP sub-waiting	27	geriatric visitors
6	GP consulting	28	GP social worker/health visitor
7	examination	29	telephonist
8	treatment	30	typist
9	GP secretaries	31	clinic nurses
10	lab.	32	district nurses
11	clean & dirty utilities	33	medical officers
12	interview	34	social workers
13	LHA consulting	35	LHA dental office
14	chiropody	36	LHA dental surgery
15	creche	37	recovery
16	outdoor playspace	38	GP dental office
17	creche cloaks & toilets	39	GP dental surgery
18	administrator	40	lab & darkroom
19	stores	41	store
20	disposal	42	staff cloaks
21	canteen & kitchen	43	caretaker's flat
22	conference	44	plant

Kentish Town health centre, London Borough of Camden. A large centre for two group practices and a wide range of local authority services. There are ten general practitioner consulting rooms; examination rooms are separate and communicate with a central treatment area behind the GP reception counters and records store. Consulting rooms and other offices are as far as possible of similar size to facilitate interchangeability. Accommodation on the ground floor includes reception and waiting space for the local health authority, health education, a creche, chiropody and LHA consulting and treatment rooms for a family health clinic. Dental services are upstairs, with offices for social workers, health visitors and district nurses, a caretaker's flat, a medical library, conference and common room. The centre is also a base for undergraduates from the medical school of a London teaching hospital. Architect: S. A. G. Cook, London Borough of Camden

but unless they can be made adequately soundproof communicating doors can create problems when there are patients in adjoining rooms simultaneously. Some people consider it best to avoid communicating doors altogether.

Other rooms

Treatment rooms should be easily accessible from both the main waiting space and the consulting rooms. The extent and nature of the other accommodation, in addition to the basic consulting suites and the essential staff rooms, lavatories, cleaners' rooms and storage, differs according to the service provided by the local authority at a particular centre, but it will almost certainly include some class space for larger group activities or lectures. These activities do not usually occur at the same time as the major clinical sessions when many people are waiting and can generally be served by a room capable of use in conjunction with the main waiting space if the activity demands it. The minimum size of class space should be large enough for about twelve ante-natal patients to lie on the floor on mattresses during relaxation sessions. It should be near the main entrance so that people do not need to stray into the rest of the building when it is not in use.

Other accommodation may include a variety of offices, interview rooms or suites for specialised purposes. These may include offices for health visitors, midwives and social workers; treatment rooms for chiropodists; rooms for school health services (e.g. ophthalmology, speech therapy or audiology); dental suites comprising separate waiting rooms, dental surgeries, recovery rooms and perhaps a dental workshop.

Again there is much to be said in the interests of flexibility for planning these to a standard useful size where this is possible. People visiting any of these will usually arrive at the centre's reception point in the first instance and will be directed to subsidiary waiting spaces if appropriate. In large centres, dental patients, although coming in through the main entrance, are likely to go to a separate reception and records point under the control of the dental practice.

Siting of the building

A small health centre can often be arranged in a single storey building. Larger health centres will tend to be situated in urban areas where site space may be restricted and more than one floor is necessary. In these cases the parts of the building visited by patients should almost certainly not exceed two floors and a passenger lift large enough for a wheelchair is needed. This is essential if any of the general practitioners' consulting suites have to be on the upper floor.

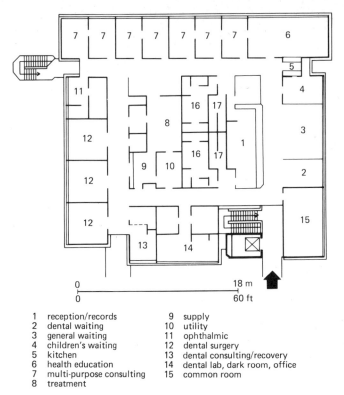

1	reception/records	9	supply
2	dental waiting	10	utility
3	general waiting	11	ophthalmic
4	children's waiting	12	dental surgery
5	kitchen	13	dental consulting/recovery
6	health education	14	dental lab, dark room, office
7	multi-purpose consulting	15	common room
8	treatment		

Lakeside health centre, Thamesmead. A local centre built to serve the first completed area of the new town. Accommodation used by patients is on an upper floor and approached from a pedestrian deck where there is a pram shelter. A continuous band of dental rooms and multi-purpose rooms encloses a central core containing reception and records, treatment space and lavatories. One sub-divided reception and waiting area serves the whole building. The intention of the plan was to encourage the integration of general practitioners and local authority health workers by providing relatively undifferentiated areas, but separate territories are usually preferred. Architects: Derek Stow and Partners

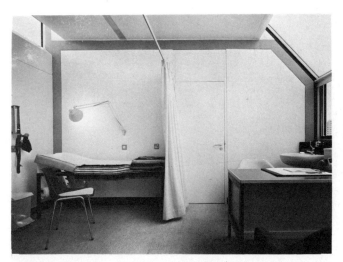

Lakeside health centre. A combined consulting/examination room, with an intercommunicating door to the adjoining consulting room. The sloping window has light-diffusing glass. (Photo: Richard Einzig)

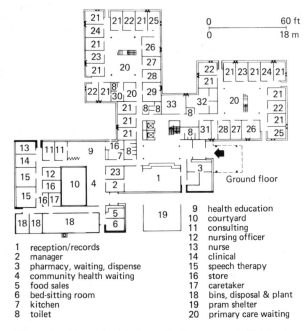

21	consulting/examination	36	void
22	health visitor	37	dental surgery
23	interview	38	recovery
24	social worker	39	x-ray
25	seminar	40	dark room
26	midwife	41	office
27	psychiatric nurse	42	staff room
28	secretaries	43	dental lab.
29	fieldwork teacher	44	staff common room
30	specimens	45	academic reception/secretaries
31	nurses service room	46	lockers
32	treatment	47	tutorial staff
33	chiropody	48	research worker
34	dental reception	49	lab.
35	dental waiting	50	preparation

9 health education
10 courtyard
11 consulting
12 nursing officer
13 nurse
14 clinical
15 speech therapy
16 store
17 caretaker
18 bins, disposal & plant
19 pram shelter
20 primary care waiting

1 reception/records
2 manager
3 pharmacy, waiting, dispense
4 community health waiting
5 food sales
6 bed-sitting room
7 kitchen
8 toilet

The projected area health centre for Thamesmead. Unlike the earlier Lakeside local centre the territories for the different units are clearly defined, but linked to one another. On the entrance floor two primary care units for group practices (sharing some central facilities) and the

local authority's community health accommodation form three distinct entities with their own waiting areas. Upstairs one unit is for dental services and the other provides tutorial and research accommodation for a London teaching hospital. Architects: Derek Stow and Partners

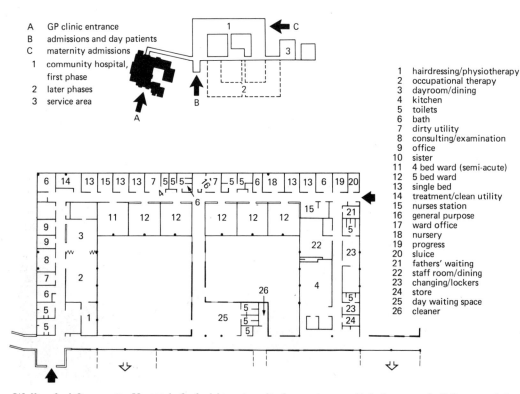

A GP clinic entrance
B admissions and day patients
C maternity admissions
1 community hospital, first phase
2 later phases
3 service area

1 hairdressing/physiotherapy
2 occupational therapy
3 dayroom/dining
4 kitchen
5 toilets
6 bath
7 dirty utility
8 consulting/examination
9 office
10 sister
11 4 bed ward (semi-acute)
12 5 bed ward
13 single bed
14 treatment/clean utility
15 nurses station
16 general purpose
17 ward office
18 nursery
19 progress
20 sluice
21 fathers' waiting
22 staff room/dining
23 changing/lockers
24 store
25 day waiting space
26 cleaner

Wallingford Community Hospital, Oxfordshire. A medical centre in a converted building houses the consulting rooms for local general practitioners, X-ray and dental suites, nursing and administrative offices, and some bedsitting rooms for resident staff and students. It is

linked to a new building containing a Day Care unit and seventeen medical and seventeen maternity beds, with provision for expansion. Architect: A. L. Arschavir, Oxford Regional Health Authority

It would probably be generally agreed, however, that whenever possible not only should the rooms of each group practice be arranged as a suite to retain the team's identity, but different practices should not be too widely separated, particularly by a floor, if they are to be encouraged to work together. If some accommodation has to be less easily accessible it is preferable to separate functions like chiropody or dentistry rather than a part of the general medical practice. If there has to be a lift it is an advantage if it is situated where it can be easily supervised from the central reception point at the entrance to the building.

Some health centres have been sited in the grounds of a district general or a community hospital. This can encourage and facilitate closer liaison between consultants and general practitioners, although this benefit by no means follows automatically. It can move some of the consultant out-patient services from the hospital to the centre, and the centre can be supported by the special diagnostic and treatment services of the hospital.

Most health centres serve smaller catchment areas remote from a hospital and such proximity is relatively rare. The essential factor in their siting is that people should be able to reach them comparatively easily on foot or by public transport; a desirable feature is that the centre should be integrated with the local community, perhaps near the shopping centre, market or library. If there is no dispensary in the health centre it is helpful if there is one nearby (such as a chemist's shop in Britain). As to their architectural character, the most important thing is probably that they should be as welcoming and domestic in scale as possible, whatever their size, rather than imposing or unnecessarily clinical in atmosphere.

The community hospital

In Britain the first resort of most people is to their local doctor. With a well-established foundation of general practitioners and of para medical and other primary care workers, local co-ordination between them can be encouraged on a national basis. A network of fairly satisfactory health centres can be created, albeit gradually and with varying degrees of integration and usually in urban areas.

However, the gap between local doctor or health centre and the relatively large and remote district general hospital is a wide one. It can be a big step, both geographically and psychologically, for the patient who has to cross it and once across he is cut off from the support of his general practitioner until he returns to his care after discharge. Although it has not yet been of high priority in the National Health

Service, possibly for economic reasons as much as anything, there are indications that it is becoming increasingly recognised that it is desirable to fill this gap. This is one purpose of what has come to be called the community hospital.

The community hospital, as the name implies, is conceived as an extension of general practice and of the primary care team rather than as a devolutionary activity of the district general hospital. Ideally it is an extension of the health centre, both functionally and geographically. It is non-specialised and in many ways is similar to the old voluntary cottage hospital run by family practitioners. Its purpose is to provide nursing care for those who for one reason or another are not in need of the more elaborate facilities of the large hospital.

For many patients it can thus be a half-way house, in whichever direction they are travelling. For example, some may be admitted by their general practitioner for straightforward child-birth or for uncomplicated non-acute disabilities where home nursing is inappropriate or cannot be arranged; others may be post-operative cases from a district general hospital who would otherwise not be ready to leave and return home. In either case, besides providing local support at a scale appropriate to the patient's disability, the community hospital can help to make it possible for the expensive beds in the more specialised hospital to be released for those who are in greater need of them. It has been argued that as high a proportion as one quarter of all hospital beds could be provided in community hospitals.

Part of a community hospital may be reserved for elderly people who need constant nursing care and who might otherwise be taken to a hospital too far removed from their home environment and from relatives and friends, but this presents the obvious danger that it could lead to an immovable population of longstay patients. A few beds may also be available as short term 'rest beds' for acute psychiatric cases under the care of a local doctor, for instance for a nervous breakdown or when a patient cannot for some reason stay at home.

Besides providing beds a community hospital can fulfil the role of a day hospital, particularly in the field of non-specialist rehabilitation therapy. For day-patients it can reduce the burden of long travelling distances and for some of them the reluctance they may feel when faced with a larger and less personal establishment. Again it can reduce the load on the large hospital.

The nature and amount of accommodation that a community hospital provides will clearly vary from one locality to another and will depend upon local needs and policy. The accommodation is likely to be

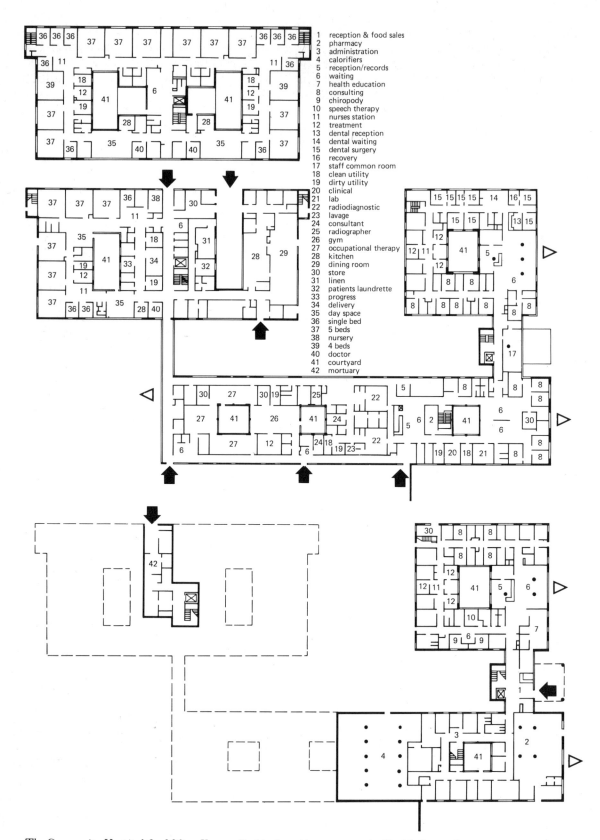

1 reception & food sales
2 pharmacy
3 administration
4 calorifiers
5 reception/records
6 waiting
7 health education
8 consulting
9 chiropody
10 speech therapy
11 nurses station
12 treatment
13 dental reception
14 dental waiting
15 dental surgery
16 recovery
17 staff common room
18 clean utility
19 dirty utility
20 clinical
21 lab
22 radiodiagnostic
23 lavage
24 consultant
25 radiographer
26 gym
27 occupational therapy
28 kitchen
29 dining room
30 store
31 linen
32 patients laundrette
33 progress
34 delivery
35 day space
36 single bed
37 5 beds
38 nursery
39 4 beds
40 doctor
41 courtyard
42 mortuary

The Community Hospital for Milton Keynes, Buckinghamshire. Three linked units comprise Health Centre, two thirty-four bed wards and thirty-three maternity beds, and a Day Hospital with relatively large out-patient, radiodiagnostic and rehabilitation departments. In the Health Centre there are separate examination rooms adjacent to the consulting rooms and a variety of offices for health visitors, social workers and home nurses etc. Architect: A. L. Arschavir, Oxford Regional Health Authority*

basically ward accommodation with a small proportion of single rooms supported by the normal ward ancillaries, with spaces for dayroom, dining, occupational therapy and physiotherapy, offices, kitchen, and rooms for staff, including dining and changing. Throughout the building it is probably even more important than it is in the normal hospital to recognise that many patients will be ambulant, or should be encouraged to be so, and that the design should facilitate this in any way it can. Day-patients will need a waiting or common room area of their own, together with separate lavatories, and may of course generate other needs according to the extent of the services it is decided to provide for them.

Work by the Oxford Regional Hospital Board suggests that the day accommodation, principally for the elderly, physically handicapped or mentally ill, may best be run in small groups of not more than twenty (fifteen patients and five staff) each with its own day room as a social centre and its own room for occupational and physiotherapy, but sharing baths, toilets and dining space with other groups.

Geriatric day hospitals

In the developed world, where the birthrate tends to be either declining or fairly static and preventive and curative medicine extends the expectation of life, there is a relatively high proportion of elderly people who are subject to the chronic and irreversible changes of old age. Inevitably there are those who need medical care and nursing in an institution, some as long-stay patients.

Many others, including the disabled and those recovering from illness, are able to live in their own homes as members of the community, or in homes for the elderly, and are sufficiently mobile to visit a day unit and benefit from organised therapy which can help them to cope with their disabilities and to manage their everyday tasks. A few elderly people may be able to reach such a unit independently but most are collected at their homes and returned to them at the end of the day in small 'buses provided by the ambulance service or by volunteers using their own transport.

Day facilities for this purpose in Britain are normally attached to general hospitals; but they are usually built as separate units with their own identity, not merely because they may be new extensions to an existing establishment but principally because in function and atmosphere they profit from a sense of independence. They are likely to provide places for about fifty elderly people and to work a five-day week. In addition to medical attention they offer physiotherapy and occupational therapy, the opportunity for

chiropody and hairdressing, sociability and mutual assistance and a communal meal. On a small and relatively domestic scale, with particular attention to the needs of the elderly, the accommodation they provide is not unlike that of the department of physical medicine in a general hospital.

The form that the accommodation takes may vary, from a simple central area for the communal activities of dining and occupational therapy around which are grouped the individual rooms for specialised functions, to more complex configurations in which the communal spaces are broken down into a variety of areas for relatively small groups of people.

Whatever the arrangements the space for physiotherapy is likely to be separated to some extent and to comprise both an open floor for exercises and some bays for individual treatment. Amongst the smaller specialised rooms there is usually a flat with bedroom, kitchen and bathroom where everyday domestic jobs can be relearnt. Toilets need to be well distributed and easy to reach, large enough for wheelchair use and for staff to help a patient, with outward opening doors. An assisted bath is essential.

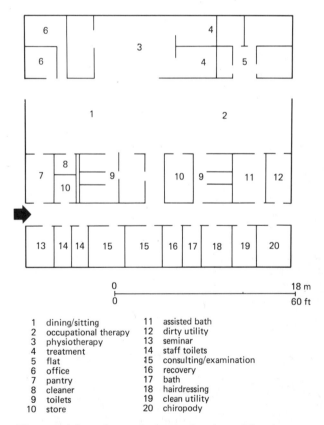

1 dining/sitting	11 assisted bath
2 occupational therapy	12 dirty utility
3 physiotherapy	13 seminar
4 treatment	14 staff toilets
5 flat	15 consulting/examination
6 office	16 recovery
7 pantry	17 bath
8 cleaner	18 hairdressing
9 toilets	19 clean utility
10 store	20 chiropody

The ground floor of a standard geriatric unit providing day accommodation for fifty patients (with inpatient accommodation on the upper floor). Vertical circulation is separate, outside the entrance, designed to suit the requirements of the particular site, and can if necessary form the link to a second unit. Architect: R. G. Brown, North Western Regional Health Authority

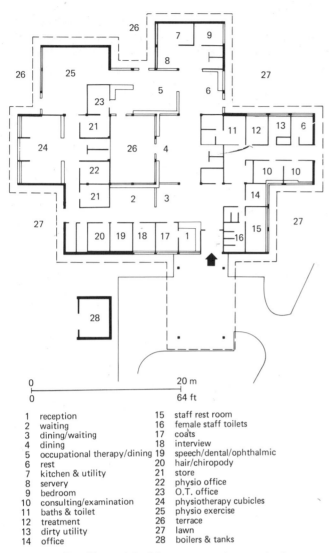

Ellesmere Day Hospital. The occupational therapy area, with the central courtyard on the right. (Photo: Richard Einzig)

1	reception	15	staff rest room
2	waiting	16	female staff toilets
3	dining/waiting	17	coats
4	dining	18	interview
5	occupational therapy/dining	19	speech/dental/ophthalmic
6	rest	20	hair/chiropody
7	kitchen & utility	21	store
8	servery	22	physio office
9	bedroom	23	O.T. office
10	consulting/examination	24	physiotherapy cubicles
11	baths & toilet	25	physio exercise
12	treatment	26	terrace
13	dirty utility	27	lawn
14	office	28	boilers & tanks

A geriatric Day Hospital for fifty patients in the grounds of Ellesmere hospital, Walton-on-Thames. Four zones for different activities are arranged around a small central courtyard, with access to sheltered lawns and terraces outside the building. Except for the areas for individual therapy, physio exercise and clinical work the circulation space, although defined, is not separated from the relatively intimate bays which adjoin it. Architects: Derek Stow and Partners

Ellesmere Day Hospital. The main entrance, with a large canopy to shelter patients arriving and departing by ambulance. (Photo: Richard Einzig)

Primary care in developing countries

In the UK there has been an attempt to provide a centrally co-ordinated health service which is available to all. This has been built up within a complicated inherited structure of medical and social services and a developed and largely urban industrialised society. However, it is clear that although advances have been made in the last quarter of a century there remain many difficulties and many differences of opinion about priorities, both theoretical and financial. There are also many different views about how best to design buildings that can help the people who work in them to do their jobs well and encourage the patients who visit them to find them agreeable.

In some other parts of the world the needs are more basic and the available resources of finance and manpower are very much smaller. Here problems of a different nature have to be overcome. Some countries are starting from almost nothing in their attempt to provide a health service for the community as a whole, and their problems have to be seen in a different context although the elements that will go towards their solution are perhaps not very different in principle from those in a developed country. The skeleton of the basic hierarchy of health care may well be similar but the organs and flesh are simpler, sometimes even rudimentary, and can only grow and develop with time.

In most developing countries health care must advance on a broad front towards an increased awareness in the community of some of the reasons for disease. These may include domestic causes such as

than in the developed world to perform the vital function of education and guidance in the community. But it is likely that the more effectively it can perform its medical and curative functions the more rapidly the community it serves will grow to trust it and co-operate in its longer term aims.

The 'aid post'

It has been argued that, in rural areas, the first unit of medical care should be an individual in every village with a little basic medical skill. This person may not necessarily be a full-time employee, but perhaps the indigenous midwife who might have a few drugs and

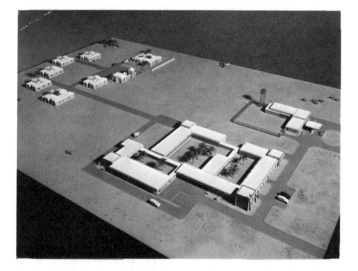

Preliminary model of the Tribal administrative Centre at Haima; an administrative, educational and health facility in the desert region of the Sultanate of Oman. The Centre is in the foreground and comprises, top left, the school; right, administration; bottom left, the medical centre. The three elements are separated by courtyards. Outlying buildings are residential villas and the guardhouse and prison. Architects: John R. Harris Associates (Photo: Sydney W. Newbery)

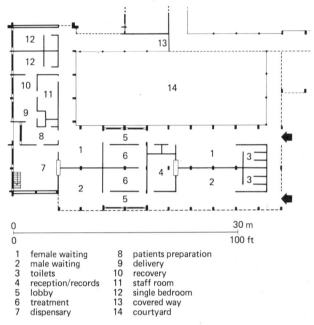

0		30 m
0		100 ft

1	female waiting	8	patients preparation
2	male waiting	9	delivery
3	toilets	10	recovery
4	reception/records	11	staff room
5	lobby	12	single bedroom
6	treatment	13	covered way
7	dispensary	14	courtyard

The medical centre at Haima. There is complete segregation of the sexes but the two treatment rooms intercommunicate. To deal with emergencies the female zone has a small delivery and recovery ward adjoining a single bedroom

contaminated water, lack of facilities for drainage, the disposal of waste, lack of care for personal hygiene and the storage, handling and preparation of food.

There is a need to improve the economy, to change social habits and to provide the material means to assist this change where possible. Nutrition, environmental health, family planning, maternity and child health and the control of communicable diseases are fundamental, and the provision of medical care can make little progress without a background of programmes of preventive care, housing and education.

Besides providing elementary medical attention a health service in a developing country, and particularly in a rural area, has thus to a much greater extent

dressings and whose primary purpose should be to spread an understanding of hygiene and elementary health care. The most simple actual establishment that needs a building, which would not be found in every village, is likely to be an 'aid post'. Probably this will not be staffed continuously but visited perhaps once a week by a para-medical assistant who might see about a hundred patients on each visit and might be assisted by a nurse.

Although it is potentially a good deal more than a first-aid post the requirements of such a building are likely to be very simple. Its construction will probably be in the vernacular, carried out by the local community, or perhaps in a mixture of indigenous and prefabricated 'imported' materials if resources, transport and skills are available.

In some communities it is likely to be an advantage if in character the building follows local tradition rather than introduces an alien atmosphere. But however simple the 'aid post' may be to begin with, if it is provided within a national or regional plan for health care it may well be conceived as the first element of a larger unit. In the future it may need to be expanded to provide additional facilities.

In the first instance the accommodation may consist of little more than a room for examination and treatment approached from an open waiting space in the form of a sheltered verandah. Even in a facility

such as this careful provision for the security of drugs will be essential. This is partly an administrative matter but the design of the building and its equipment must recognise it, for security of drugs can be a major problem in developing countries, as indeed it has proved to be elsewhere.

The simple form of building to meet these needs is little more than a hut. This can be seen in a slightly larger form in the Sudanese proposals for primary health care units. An extension might add more space for examination or treatment, a dispensary, a small laboratory and an expanded waiting area, or separate facilities for records and space for health education and more staff. Later extension might provide some beds. The nature of growth depends on local needs but it is likely to be important that growth should be foreseen. It should not be inhibited by a nucleus from which it cannot easily develop or which can only be adapted by alterations so radical that, when change is needed, the facility is put out of action. Throughout the world, education and an increase in wealth, however slight, is always followed by increasing public demand for better health care.

Development of the small unit
Growth will probably anticipate three roles: an increase in the curative treatment of out-patients, the provision of beds, and the co-ordination of public

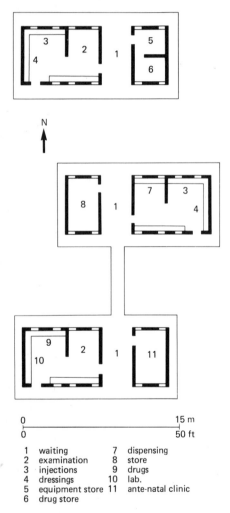

1	waiting	7	dispensing
2	examination	8	store
3	injections	9	drugs
4	dressings	10	lab.
5	equipment store	11	ante-natal clinic
6	drug store		

A model plan (top) for a Primary Health Care Unit in the 78/84 National Health Programme for the Sudan. Staffed by one primary health care worker it is intended to serve a population of 4000 within a radius of attendance of about 16 km or 10 miles. It is capable of future extension into a dispensary (bottom) by the addition of a second building. A dispensary for referral, supervision and the supply of drugs should serve five Primary Health Care Units and a population of 24 000, staffed by a medical assistant, a nurse and a cleaner

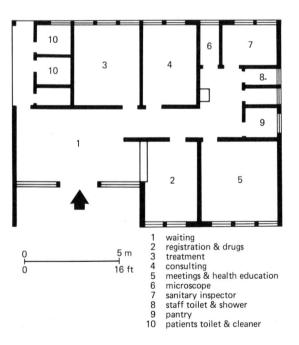

1	waiting
2	registration & drugs
3	treatment
4	consulting
5	meetings & health education
6	microscope
7	sanitary inspector
8	staff toilet & shower
9	pantry
10	patients toilet & cleaner

A rural health centre to serve a community of less than 2500 inhabitants. It is staffed by one health worker visited about once a week by a mobile team of doctor, nurse, sanitarian and health educator. Architect: Abou Zeid Rageh, Cairo (with acknowledgement to WHO)

health services in the improvement of general health and preventive action against social diseases. The type of provision that is made for the development of a basic unit into a small hospital will depend largely on the nature of the catchment area, on the living conditions of the community and their particular demands, on the prevalence of specific diseases, and also on its cultural acceptability. For example, in most areas it is likely to be the out-patient clinics and the distribution of medicines that have priority. In other areas, where the rate of infant mortality is high, the provision of wards for infants may come first; or where living conditions and social habits particularly endanger childbirth a maternity ward may be more important. Elsewhere a few general beds for men and women may be all that is possible.

Whatever the initial assessment of need it is likely that with time the situation will change. The basic unit should allow not only for expansion but should also permit some flexibility for changes in use and for variations in the relative numbers of beds for men and women. This is a factor that can affect the plan fundamentally, particularly in those parts of the world where strict segregation is necessary.

Staffing and equipment
Whatever the size of the facility it is almost certain that, compared with the western health centre or community hospital, it will be run by a much smaller staff and that there will be less specialisation of tasks.

1 waiting & meeting room
2 medicines
3 injections & vaccinations
4 consulting
5 store
6 toilet
7 sitting/dining room
8 bedroom
9 kitchen & clothes yard
10 dentisty
11 information/records
12 health inspector
13 office
14 emergencies
15 obstetric beds
16 adult beds

17 childrens beds
18 kitchen
19 laundry
20 delivery
21 labour
22 doctors changing & toilet
23 clean utility/sterilization
24 dirty utility
25 nurses station
26 visitors
27 nurse's bedroom

Designs from Columbia for the National Hospital Fund, produced as an aid to the planning of health posts and health centres. The basic unit of the model health post (top), with separate staff living quarters, is first extended without significant alteration to provide for dentistry and offices (centre). Another building can subsequently be added (bottom) with labour and delivery rooms, pairs of beds for adults, children and obstetric patients, and a self-contained nurse's bedroom. Architect: Jorge de los Rios Mazure, Bogota (with acknowledgement to WHO)

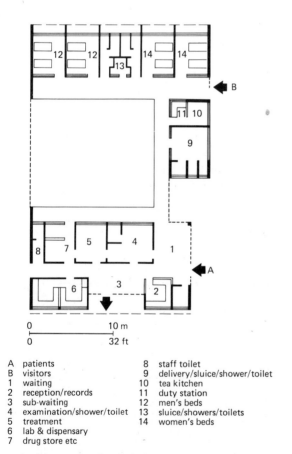

0 — 10 m
0 — 32 ft

A patients
B visitors
1 waiting
2 reception/records
3 sub-waiting
4 examination/shower/toilet
5 treatment
6 lab & dispensary
7 drug store etc
8 staff toilet
9 delivery/sluice/shower/toilet
10 tea kitchen
11 duty station
12 men's beds
13 sluice/showers/toilets
14 women's beds

A health centre with eight beds and delivery room, with an outpatient capacity of up to one hundred patients a day. Staffed by two or three nurses/midwives and an administrator, it is visited periodically by a mobile health team. Inpatients are cared for by their relatives. Architects: Misereor, Aachen (with acknowledgement to WHO)

Equipment will also be simpler and indeed it is important that it is of the simplest, as skilled maintenance will not usually be available. In the absence of country doctors it will probably be the only centre within many miles to which people can turn. Patients will not come by appointment but are likely to arrive on foot or in bullock carts, sometimes with their families and even with their livestock. If their treatment involves a number of consecutive visits, for example for dressings, injections or follow-up after diagnostic tests, they are unlikely to return home

between treatments if the journey takes several days but may camp in the vicinity.

Even in areas where the facility is a short distance from patients' homes, and even in a town where there may possibly be an appointment system, patients are likely to arrive very early in the morning although it may involve them in waiting in large numbers for many hours in uncomfortable climatic conditions. Out-patient clinics will thus be dealing with a situation very different from that which is usual in an urbanised western society. In the wards, admission may mean that other members of the family will stay nearby and will play an important part in cooking for and generally looking after the patient. The admission of a small child to a bed will be likely to involve admitting the mother as well.

There are examples, notably in Africa, where provision is made for this influx of patients' families by the construction nearby of a hospital village or of simple hostels. Besides sheltering the relatives of the sick this accommodation can be used by non-infectious patients who are capable of looking after themselves. Such self-care patients may constitute a substantial proportion and deliberately organised residential shelter of this kind can considerably reduce the number who might otherwise be occupying hospital beds that require nursing attendance.

The larger health centres or out-patient departments in rural areas are likely to be manned by several auxiliaries but by only one doctor. In these circumstances a method of sorting patients into those who need only routine treatment or medicines and those who should be seen by the doctor may be necessary.

A simple arrangement based on a sorting method and one-way traffic, derived from French experience in West Africa, is for patients to wait on a covered verandah and to enter a long hut-like building at one

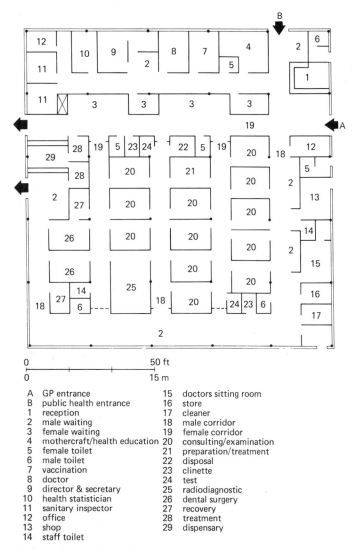

A	GP entrance	15	doctors sitting room
B	public health entrance	16	store
1	reception	17	cleaner
2	male waiting	18	male corridor
3	female waiting	19	female corridor
4	mothercraft/health education	20	consulting/examination
5	female toilet	21	preparation/treatment
6	male toilet	22	disposal
7	vaccination	23	clinette
8	doctor	24	test
9	director & secretary	25	radiodiagnostic
10	health statistician	26	dental surgery
11	sanitary inspector	27	recovery
12	office	28	treatment
13	shop	29	dispensary
14	staff toilet		

A general practitioners' clinic for use in association with a new hospital in the Middle East where there are as yet relatively few primary health care facilities. To avoid pressure and overcrowding in the outpatient department it is intended to act as a filter for referral. The strict segregation of the sexes produces an interlocking finger arrangement of independent corridors, but all consulting rooms communicate with both men's and women's corridors so that clinics can respond to variations in numbers. Architects: Architects' Co-Partnership

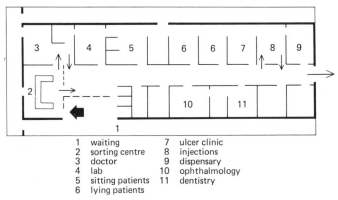

1	waiting	7	ulcer clinic
2	sorting centre	8	injections
3	doctor	9	dispensary
4	lab	10	ophthalmology
5	sitting patients	11	dentistry
6	lying patients		

Diagrammatic plan (after G. Ferrand) for an outpatients department. Patients are filtered at the sorting centre and proceed either to the doctor's room or along the corridor to the various clinics, leaving the building at the other end after passing the dispensary

end, where they are seen by a medical assistant at a sorting and records point. Those who need to visit the doctor are directed to an immediately adjoining doctor's room, but the majority are passed into a corridor that runs the length of the building, from which they distribute themselves into the various clinics and wait for treatment. All patients leave the building by way of the same corridor at the end remote from the entrance, passing a dispensary on their way out. Between the clinics there is access for staff, independent of the patients' corridor, from the doctor's room at one end to the dispensary at the other.

Wards and service rooms

If there are wards they are likely to be of the open type, particularly if nursing staff is limited in number. In addition there should be two or three rooms for

isolation. In a small facility with only one nursing unit of perhaps twenty-five to thirty beds it may be sensible to place the service rooms at the centre so that the ward is divided into separate sections for men and women, or for other purposes for which segregation is desirable, whilst maintaining in principle one nursing unit. Smaller multi-bed bays may give greater flexibility in use but their adoption needs to be balanced against the degree of supervision that is desirable.

Service rooms will probably be reduced to essentials – a treatment room, a workroom for cleaning instruments, sterilisation and preparation, a ward kitchen or pantry, some storage space and offices for a nurse and doctor. Separate lavatories will be necessary for each sex, but unlike the dispersed and individual facilities that are favoured in the West, these are probably best concentrated together so that they are easy to supervise and keep clean. Also, in some climates, a

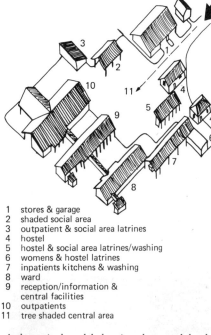

1 stores & garage
2 shaded social area
3 outpatient & social area latrines
4 hostel
5 hostel & social area latrines/washing
6 womens & hostel latrines
7 inpatients kitchens & washing
8 ward
9 reception/information & central facilities
10 outpatients
11 tree shaded central area

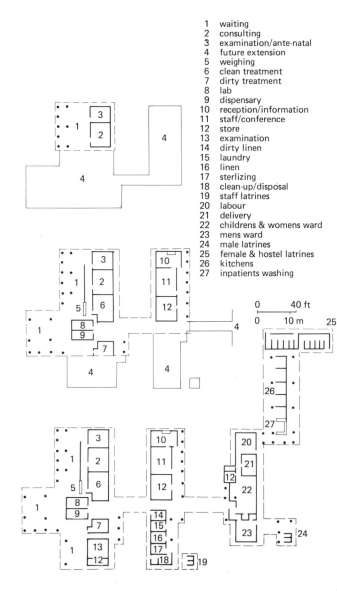

1 waiting
2 consulting
3 examination/ante-natal
4 future extension
5 weighing
6 clean treatment
7 dirty treatment
8 lab
9 dispensary
10 reception/information
11 staff/conference
12 store
13 examination
14 dirty linen
15 laundry
16 linen
17 sterlizing
18 clean-up/disposal
19 staff latrines
20 labour
21 delivery
22 childrens & womens ward
23 mens ward
24 male latrines
25 female & hostel latrines
26 kitchens
27 inpatients washing

0   40 ft
0   10 m   25

A theoretical model showing the staged development from a small clinic into a well supported health centre to serve a population of up to 20 000 within a radius of ten to twenty miles. Within the context of an overall development there can be many variations on the theme to suit local needs and conditions. The example shows (top) an under-fives general clinic. It is enlarged (centre) into a bigger clinic with ancillary rooms and more space for staff and storage. It is further extended (bottom) to provide maternity facilities and a few beds for men. Later extensions might enlarge it by increments of twenty-five beds into a 125-bed District Hospital. There is provision for hostels or dormitories for relatives and self-care patients, and for places where they can do their cooking and laundry. The plans assume that there is unlikely to be waterborne sewage. Architect: Mark Wells, with the Medical Committee of the Conference of Missionary Societies of Great Britain and Ireland

degree of separation from the ward may be desirable for reasons of hygiene.

Lavatories may be combined with simple slop sink facilities for emptying bedpans. Day space may best be provided in the form of covered verandahs opening directly off the ward. This arrangement, in single-storey buildings, may be particularly suitable in giving easy access for visitors and patients' families without interfering with the work centre of the ward.

A theoretical example which by stages extends a simple health post by the addition, first of further clinics and supporting facilities and subsequently of in-patient beds, was produced in 1975 by the Medical Committee of the Conference of Missionary Societies in Great Britain and Ireland. It is not, nor is it intended to be, a model for all situations, but in addition to the practicality of its suggestions about the way growth might be guided, it demonstrates a design approach that pays regard to the rural culture and social habits of many tropical countries in the developing world. This approach is more relevant, sympathetic, and far simpler to implement than some of the sophisticated solutions, often entirely in-appropriate, that are based on the experience of the western world and misapplied to totally different situations.

This does not mean that there are no situations where more sophisticated answers are appropriate. The World Health Organisation has published examples from contributors which, although simple in conception, assume a less primitive technology and different social habits. However, these usually share an approach that anticipates growth and provides for it by the simple addition of linked units or 'huts' in structures of one storey.

Prefabricated and mobile services

Some attempts have been made to explore the possibilities of prefabricated units. These may have uses where local materials are not readily available or suitable local labour is for one reason or another difficult to obtain, or speed of implementation is of particular importance. However, this is a relatively costly approach and in most situations is likely to be out of scale with the essential needs. But given, for instance, a large programme and reasonable facilities for transport, together with the necessary finance, there seems little to be said against it except that by its very nature it imports an entirely alien artefact into the community. Yet since any community that can be easily reached by the sort of vehicle necessary to transport prefabricated buildings will probably already be familiar with alien artefacts and may, indeed, place a higher social value upon them than upon its own vernacular, this may be no argument against their use.

In countries which can afford them (e.g. Qatar) fully prefabricated imported buildings which can be erected rapidly by a few skilled expatriates,who then return home, are preferred to traditional methods of construction which require large numbers of imported unskilled labourers who stay in the country for a long time and disturb its culture.

In other situations an approach more relevant than the completely prefabricated building may be the

The treatment room in one of the containerised units at Thamesmead, delivered complete except for the loose equipment. (Photo: Richard Einzig)

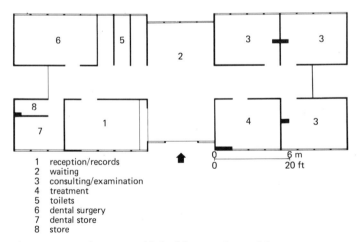

1 reception/records
2 waiting
3 consulting/examination
4 treatment
5 toilets
6 dental surgery
7 dental store
8 store

A temporary and transportable health centre designed for use in different locations during the growth of the new community at Thamesmead. Four units of container size suitable for loading on vehicles, complete with all their internal fittings, were linked together on site by pre-fabricated roofs and floors forming the waiting space and corridors. Architects: Derek Stow and Partners

importation of simple structural members which can then be enclosed by local labour with an adaptation of the materials and methods that are normally available in the locality. This may also prove to be more flexible and more suitable for subsequent adaptations and additions than some of the more fully prefabricated products which are difficult to modify.

An example of the fully prefabricated approach in an entirely different context, but which may be of relevance elsewhere, was the transportable health centre used in Britain at Thamesmead in South London when the new community was in the early years of construction. A temporary health facility was needed in various locations as construction advanced, which would be superseded by a permanent and larger building when the town had reached a more developed stage.

The building consisted of four units of approximately container size, each capable of being loaded on a vehicle. The units were structurally self-sufficient and complete with doors, windows and all services and fitted installations. They were linked together on site by prefabricated flooring, cladding and roofing which formed the waiting and circulation areas, where there were no requirements for servicing. Given the availability of incoming and outgoing services site preparation was minimal, as was the internal work necessary to bring the building into use.

In some parts of the world 'mobile homes' have been used for housing construction staff on major projects where no existing accommodation is available. It is possible that there may be something to be learnt from them for the smaller types of health buildings, or at least for those elements of them that justify relatively sophisticated accommodation. They have the benefits of convenience and comfort, and are relatively easily transported. Although high in cost, complete factory finished units which can be easily linked together, as an alternative to prefabricated elements that have to be assembled piece by piece and fitted out by procedures similar to normal building, may sometimes be more relevant in the developing world than they have generally been found to be elsewhere.

However, since adequate staffing for a health service is usually a greater problem than suitable buildings and can take a good deal longer to provide, it may be that in most situations instant availability is not really the first priority. Where there are adequate roads mobile units are probably more relevant in the context of a mobile health service. These can travel from one district to another and give support, with more sophisticated equipment and a higher degree of scarce medical skill, to the work of isolated rural health posts far distant from the nearest hospital. In

Britain mobile transfusion units collecting blood from donors and X-ray scanning units for preventive medicine perform in their different ways an analogous function.

If communication by road is practicable it may be better to rotate a relatively high degree of service around the skeleton of a more elementary one than to attempt to build up permanent and more elaborate establishments everywhere. A service of this nature need not depend upon the use of large mobile trailers or lorries. The important thing is that the scarce and more highly skilled worker, based perhaps in the district hospital, should be available to visit and support the auxiliaries in the more remote outposts.

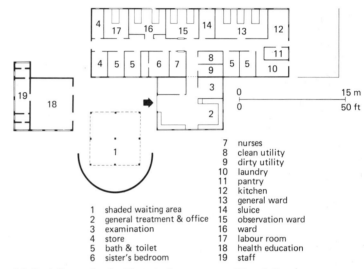

1	shaded waiting area	7	nurses
2	general treatment & office	8	clean utility
3	examination	9	dirty utility
4	store	10	laundry
5	bath & toilet	11	pantry
6	sister's bedroom	12	kitchen
		13	general ward
		14	sluice
		15	observation ward
		16	ward
		17	labour room
		18	health education
		19	staff

Medical Centre for the Aboriginal community of Ernabella in Australia, with provision for outpatient examination and treatment, seven short-stay beds and a labour room. A separate multi-purpose building is used for health education, staff meetings and training. There is a shaded open-air waiting area between the two buildings. The beds are intended as overnight accommodation or for patients awaiting transport to the base hospital. The centre is staffed by two registered nurses and two or three Aboriginal women health workers. An aerial medical service supplies a fortnightly medical clinic. The centre was constructed in Adelaide, some 900 miles away, and the parts transported by road for erection on the site. Architects: Public Buildings Department, South Australian Government

Where communications are difficult or long distances are involved a mobile health service that uses aircraft may be relevant. If China's 'barefoot doctor' is at one end of the scale the 'flying doctor' is at the other. Flying services have been used in Australia and in the Scottish Highlands but in developing countries their most significant application has probably been in connection with epidemiological surveys and mass immunisation campaigns and similar one-off projects funded with external aid.

Flying services are expensive, and are unlikely to justify themselves as a permanent element in the health facilities of a poor country, particularly if they are seen only as a means of transporting emergency patients over long distances to a centre which is equipped to deal with them or in bringing a doctor to an emergency. Where a country can afford a flying service of any sort it is more likely to be of value in carrying specialist medical teams from one hospital to another for clinical sessions, where attention can be provided at a level of skill that would otherwise be completely beyond reach.

Chapter 3

The general hospital

A general hospital is one that is organised to deal with a variety of conditions of illness needing specialised skills or equipment that cannot economically be provided in the patient's home or in small medical centres in the community. It brings together in a concentrated form most of the specialist services otherwise performed by a number of separate hospitals with more limited functions – hospitals for children, for women, for accidents, for orthopaedic work or for mental illness – and it provides care for both inpatients and outpatients.

Patients normally stay in a general hospital for a relatively short time, and the building is sometimes known as a general *acute* hospital. This implies illness of rapid onset and usually of short duration, to distinguish it from a hospital whose patients are, for example, chronically ill and who are for this reason likely to be of longer stay.

Within the National Health Service in Britain, the general hospital usually supports a school of nursing, and is known as a District General Hospital because it is based on a particular catchment area.

The size of hospitals

General hospitals are often categorised by the number of beds they contain but this gives little indication of their true extent and complexity. The ancillary departments, necessary to support the beds and to deal with outpatients, have greatly increased in size and sophistication in the last quarter of a century.

Hospitals contain three basic categories of accommodation, all different in function and physical requirements. Firstly there are the beds themselves, organised in wards of a size appropriate to their speciality and the nursing teams that look after them;

to each ward is attached the accommodation necessary for its day-to-day clinical and domestic servicing. Secondly, there are the departments which provide the diagnostic, surgical, medical and therapeutic services needed to support the wards and minister to out-patients. Thirdly, there are the departments that look after the establishment as a whole, providing it with medical and domestic supplies, food and energy, and maintaining the physical fabric and equipment. The relative space occupied by these categories of accommodation varies somewhat with the type of hospital and the country in which it is situated but in a typical general hospital in a western country the total area of all the other departments may well be about equal to that of all the wards.

The size of general hospitals varies considerably, depending principally on the population of the area served. In the UK the lower limit is nowadays thought to be about 600 beds serving a population of some 100 000 and the upper limit about 900 or 1000. It is difficult, and can be misleading, to make international comparisons but although there are many instances of much smaller general hospitals (and even 300 beds constitutes quite a large establishment) this range of size seems to be fairly widely accepted, with a tendency to avoid the upper limit.

From the patient's point of view and in its public impact a hospital of a thousand or more beds can be a formidable establishment and there may be persuasive arguments on human and environmental grounds for avoiding such a size unless there are compelling reasons to justify it. Much depends upon the manner in which a complex of this magnitude is designed, and in this respect there is by no means only one type of solution. It will be appreciated that below a certain number of beds, the supporting facilities that can be economically provided will be reduced and the specialist treatment that can be readily available will be limited.

Space and standards

Although techniques for diagnosis and treatment are largely international, the space standards for individual parts of a hospital can vary widely from one country to another. Besides cultural factors and different methods of working they reflect the funds allocated for construction and equipment and the money that will be available for the recurrent costs of staff and supplies and for keeping the facility operational.

In the UK during the last quarter of a century there has been a substantial programme of hospital building, providing new facilities and replacing or extending old ones, in an attempt to keep pace with the demands of a health service available to everybody. Accompanying this programme there has been considerable operational research. Much ingenuity has been exercised in trying to eliminate wasteful space in order to keep capital and running costs within budgets and at the same time to meet clinical needs and to provide good working conditions and an improved environment for patients.

Some of the resulting space standards should be regarded as absolute minima and would not necessarily be appropriate in many parts of the world, nor indeed would some of them be acceptable. For example, in some Moslem countries the need to separate the accommodation for men and women to a much greater degree than elsewhere, and the spaces in which they circulate, can add greatly to the area of some parts of a hospital. In other contexts spaces that in Britain are considered essential may be almost irrelevant. Social customs such as hospital visiting by whole families at all hours of the day, or the supply of food to patients by relatives encamped nearby, can also have a profound influence on the type of space that is needed.

The space that is genuinely appropriate for the various components of a hospital is not always easy to determine. Sometimes it is related to the dimensions of machines or pieces of equipment, static or mobile, and to the activities performed by people around such equipment. For many such areas there are almost universal guidelines because the techniques employed are international and reasonable dimensions can be determined with some certainty if the scope of the facility and the methods of operation can be predicted. However, there are dangers in tailoring the space too precisely to fit a particular function that may alter after a few years, even before a building is occupied.

Appropriate space is also related to estimations of minimum distances for the avoidance of cross-infection, combined with social acceptability, as in the spacing of beds. Standards in western countries may be very different from those which the customs of another country permit or which are sometimes forced upon an overloaded establishment. In some circumstances it may be both unnecessary and unrealistic to plan for the arrangement of beds with curtains round each bed to give privacy during examinations or when the patient is using a bedpan. It may also be unnecessary for every patient to have both a locker and a bedside chair. People accustomed to living with their families and animals in the open air and retiring to one or two small rooms or to the roof are not likely to react in the same way as an urban western European or Northern American to what the latter might regard as a crowded ward. In a hot climate there may be a need for 'dayroom' facilities that would be entirely inappropriate elsewhere.

'Normal' solutions based on the experience of western countries can tend to become enshrined as absolutes for reasons of convenience. These solutions can come to be accepted all too readily by designers if they do not question them and enquire into the roots of the requirements and seek an appropriate answer.

Some countries are reaching a stage of development where they can build major new hospitals, perhaps for the first time in their history. Understandably they wish to provide the best available, but may be prone to the belief that standards of excellence are only to be found in models based on western patterns. They may not recognise that these standards have been produced in response to western demands and a dissimilar background.

In some countries of the developing world hospitals have been built whose relevance to the real needs of the population is doubtful in the extreme. The countries acquiring these hospitals may have no infrastructure of primary health care with which to underpin them and no adequate pool of professional and technical staff who can be recruited to run them. The installation may be an inappropriately sophisticated importation, conceived elsewhere with medical enthusiasm and commercial opportunism, and bought blindly for political reasons.

More than any other building for health care a hospital is an expensive and complicated installation and costs a great deal to keep in operation, particularly in its staffing overheads. Its design should spring, in the first instance, not from a convenient schedule of customary accommodation but from a realistic analysis of the functions it is intended to fulfil and the manner in which it can perform them.

Variously known as a 'philosophy of service' or an 'operational policy' this analysis extends to a detailed appraisal of the proposed methods of working and the procedures that are to be adopted throughout the organisation. It must anticipate the activities in every part of the establishment, both in strategic terms and in considerable tactical detail. Unless the strategy is determined at the outset no amount of subsequent adjustment in the physical planning is likely to satisfy the actual requirements.

How are patients to reach the hospital and how are they to be handled and deployed when they have got there? How are the many different categories of staff to reach it? Where are they going to change their clothes and leave their belongings and what amenities do they need during their working hours? How are the wards to be run and how are patients to be taken to the theatre or to other vital ancillary services? What are the procedures for handling specimens from their point of origin to the laboratories? How are medical and domestic supplies to be received, stored and distributed and how is food to be prepared, cooked and delivered to patients and staff? What arrangements are to be made for visitors? How is cleaning and maintenance to be performed, and refuse and infected matter to be disposed of? What actions will be necessary if there is a fire in the building?

These and many other procedures need to be thought through and determined in principle as a part of the designer's brief. Some of them may be irreconcilable in the context of the total problem and the planning solution that is possible in the particular instance; they may have to be changed or modified accordingly. It is important that these procedures should not be derived afterwards from the constraints of a building design that has been conceived in ignorance of them.

An understanding of primary requirements analogous to these is, of course, vital for the design of any building for health care, or indeed of any building for a special purpose. In the case of a hospital, the determination of the primary requirements is of particular importance because of the size, complexity and interdependence of the different parts and the universal acceptance that it should function with the maximum ease, efficiency and economy in saving human life.

In countries with a well established hospital service and a long tradition of experience and precedent the answers to some of the above questions of operational policy may be fairly conventional, in the sense that there is general agreement about a way of doing things. Much may even be codified in broad terms as a matter of national policy, not least because only then can expenditure be controlled, lengthy discussion between the various interests avoided and reasonably rapid design and construction achieved.

Even so there will from time to time be a breakthrough in one area or another demanding a reassessment of policy, altering relationships and affecting accommodation in detail. The provision of sterile supplies from a central source is a relatively recent example of this. In countries without such an established tradition a much more fundamental analysis of all aspects of operational policy is necessary if inappropriate and supposedly 'universal' assumptions are to be guarded against and strategic mistakes avoided.

General arrangement

Wherever a hospital is situated, whatever the culture and whatever its size and detailed operational policies, it will contain both wards and supporting departments. The wards may be categorised by speciality, by the sex or age of patients, and to some degree each will be run as a self-contained unit. These are considered in Chapter 4.

The supporting departments will be categorised by their speciality and the particular services they perform; each discharges a different function with its own staff and a certain amount of its own administration but many of them are closely related functionally to others. Not all departments are medical, surgical or therapeutic. Separate departments will be necessary for central administration, for the receipt and distribution of stores, for the preparation, cooking and distribution of food, for the physical maintenance of the building and its services and equipment, for heating, ventilation and other mechanical plant. The basic nature of some of the principal departments is the subject of Chapter 5.

The last half century has seen important changes in attitude towards the form that the planning of wards should take. Although opinions continue to vary and change on this matter and the solution for one society may be different from that for another, the spaces occupied by beds and their ancillary rooms are relatively finite units in a hospital. There may be fluctuations in the numbers of patients occupying beds of different specialities which may be due to seasonal changes or a reduction in the incidence of particular diseases by preventive advances or the introduction of new methods of treatment. For this reason it may be an advantage if there is some physical continuity between one ward unit and another so that one can expand by a few beds at the expense of its next door neighbour. Yet despite such minor modifications, it is improbable that wards will need to be altered in nature or size in any fundamental way during the useful life of the building. If the bed capacity of the hospital has to be increased further separate wards will be added; they are unlikely to affect the existing units.

In some of the central departments that support the wards, on the other hand, considerable changes may need to be anticipated. The relative importance of the functions they perform may alter and in some departments the space required for efficient operation may shrink or expand. In addition, the nature of the equipment and servicing may change and entirely new departments may need to be added.

The form and arrangement of the wards is fundamental and will have a major effect on the form of the whole building. However, the major strategic decisions in hospital planning will have to be taken in the relationship of the central departments to one another and to the wards. Future changes in the nature and size of the departments will have to be anticipated, as well as the the logistic arrangements for communications and supplies. The problems are complex, particularly when the initial capital cost of the building is geared to the specific accommodation that can be justified at the time it is conceived. A loose fit, which probably implies the provision of more than the minimum efficient space, cannot usually be reconciled with the budget.

The complexities are usually intensified when the building has to be designed for a restricted site and the room for manoeuvre is very limited. But even on large open sites where there is plenty of space to spread, and particularly in hospitals with more than about 500 beds, there may well be a conflict between planning in a form loose enough to provide for future change and expansion and the distances that staff and patients need to travel to get from one place to another.

Frequently there is the further complication that the hospital has to be built in stages, or is a phased extension of older buildings that are already in use. Usually the first stage and each subsequent enlargement must constitute a viable operational unit. The progressive work of construction (and perhaps modification of what has already been built) must interfere as little as possible with the function and amenity of the accommodation already occupied. Unlike most buildings a hospital is in use twenty-four hours a day on every day of the year; there are no week-end or holiday breaks during which alterations can be organised.

Form and ventilation

The total form of a hospital building and the relationships of its different parts will be influenced by many factors; one that is likely to be fundamental is the policy to be adopted for its ventilation.

Air conditioning is generally recognised as of the highest priority in the operating theatre suite. Air

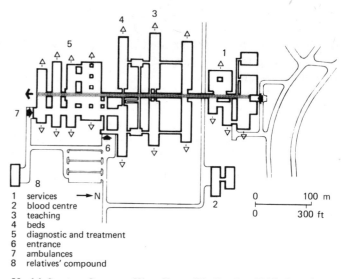

1 services
2 blood centre
3 teaching
4 beds
5 diagnostic and treatment
6 entrance
7 ambulances
8 relatives' compound

Health Services Centre at Khon Kaen, Thailand; a 580 bed teaching hospital capable of expansion to 700 beds. Designed to rely as little as possible on high technology, the buildings are naturally ventilated except in those few areas where medical needs call for air-conditioning. A central hospital street in which patient, visitor and service traffics are segregated runs through the whole complex and most departments are independently extendable. Architects: Llewelyn-Davies Weeks

The first completed ward building at Khon Kaen. Wide overhangs, sun screens and natural through-ventilation

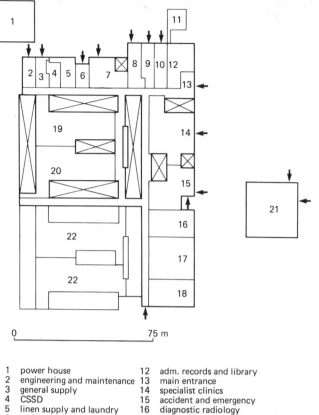

1	power house	12	adm. records and library
2	engineering and maintenance	13	main entrance
3	general supply	14	specialist clinics
4	CSSD	15	accident and emergency
5	linen supply and laundry	16	diagnostic radiology
6	staff change	17	operating
7	catering	18	delivery
8	laboratories	19	male general acute ward
9	mortuary	20	female, obstetric and childrens ward
10	pharmacy		(future male ward)
11	prayer room	21	G.P. clinic
		22	future wards

Diagrammatic plan of a single storey fifty bed fully air-conditioned hospital for Saudi Arabia, capable of expansion to one hundred beds by the addition of two ward units. All daylight to the wards is from shaded internal courtyards. Ward circulation is separated from the main L-shaped hospital street. Architects: Architects' Co-Partnership

Model of an internal courtyard for Saudi Arabian hospitals, with eggcrate louvres for the control of sunlight

conditioning in this context means the ability to control the air temperature both above and below the ambient temperature and also to control the humidity, with sterile filtration in addition. In temperate climates, in most other departments, although for medical reasons air conditioning may be be desirable, particularly in noisy and polluted urban situations, it cannot by any means be regarded as essential. It is, of course, more important in tropical countries and in hot desert areas where dust storms blow for half the year. In the wards there may be strong arguments against air conditioning, particularly when it is entirely strange to the normal habitat, customs and expectations of the patients.

An artificial environment of 'pure' air throughout the building, however well filtered and tempered, is also no guarantee against infection. Air movement can have an important bearing on the incidence of infection, especially if air removed from an infected area is blown or sucked into another part of the building through ventilation or duct systems. Unfortunately, the installation of full air treatment does not always achieve a reduction of the incidence of outbreaks of infection. Indeed, many hospitals which are dependent for their ventilation on throwing open windows and doors (the method that was understandably so vigorously recommended by Florence Nightingale) have less frequent outbreaks than those with full air conditioning. Further, not only is air conditioning expensive but it is a constant consumer of energy and an extremely demanding servant.

Unnecessary dependence on wholly artificial means of air control can impose intolerable difficulties when sophisticated systems break down and prompt and

Salmaniya Medical Centre, Bahrain; a 550 bed air-conditioned hospital. Patients' rooms face north and south to minimise solar heat gain and the relatively small window openings are deeply shaded. East and west flank walls are blank. Architects: Llewelyn-Davies Weeks. (Photo: Henk Snoek Photography & Associates)

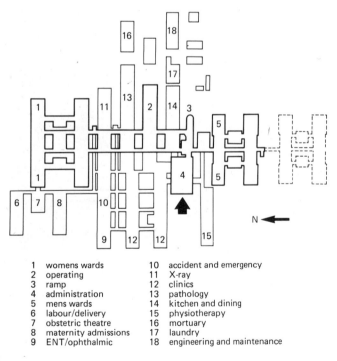

1 womens wards
2 operating
3 ramp
4 administration
5 mens wards
6 labour/delivery
7 obstetric theatre
8 maternity admissions
9 ENT/ophthalmic
10 accident and emergency
11 X-ray
12 clinics
13 pathology
14 kitchen and dining
15 physiotherapy
16 mortuary
17 laundry
18 engineering and maintenance

Preliminary model of Maiduguri Teaching Hospital in NE Nigeria, a hot dry region bordering on the Sahara. Separate fingers of accommodation face north and south and the ward areas are naturally ventilated and deeply shaded. Architect: John R Harris. (Photo: Henk Snoek Photography & Associates)

The 517 bed Maiduguri Teaching Hospital in the hot dry region of NE Nigeria, a Moslem area. Men's and women's wards are at opposite ends of the two storey spine, from which long fingers enclosing courtyards are developed outwards on the lower floor. A possible future extension to the south could provide a further 256 beds. Wards are naturally ventilated, theatres and ITU fully air conditioned, certain other areas such as offices are air conditioned with local window mounted units, and some rooms such as clean and dirty utilities are mechanically ventilated. Teaching accommodation is distributed in blocks throughout the building, mostly on the upper floor. Architect: John R Harris

efficient maintenance cannot be relied upon. Total dependence upon it can quickly render a building uninhabitable in such circumstances.

Whether in a temperate or tropical climate total air conditioning makes possible a high ratio of internal space to external wall and permits a compact building form that would be entirely impracticable without it. Air conditioning may thus reduce the site area that is necessary and will tend to lead to economy in the cost of the actual fabric of the building, but not to that of its artificial lighting and other services or of its maintenance. Conversely, reliance on natural ventilation will impose inescapable constraints on the shape that the plan can take. Because natural ventilation will produce a relatively high ratio of external wall to floor area it will be likely to increase the cost of the building fabric although reducing that of its services and running costs.

Whatever the policy regarding ventilation, however, it is well to recognise that some forms of planning, particularly in multi-storey buildings, may make air conditioning essential. Even in temperate climates any block of accommodation with a depth of more than about 15 m which contains internal rooms is unlikely to be able to rely satisfactorily on natural ventilation, even when supplemented artificially. This is particularly true of internal rooms which generate heat from equipment. The building will need to be air conditioned if the temperature in the core of the block is to be prevented from rising above the ambient and a healthy and acceptable working environment is to be maintained.

The form that a naturally ventilated hospital can take will be affected by the climate, but in tropical countries it will be dominated by it. In the warm humid regions, about 15° north and south of the Equator, free air movement through relatively shallow ranges of building is vital for comfort. In these locations it is desirable to plan for the maximum exposure of occupied spaces to the prevailing wind that is compatible with shading from the sun, and also to separate parallel blocks of building sufficiently widely not to shelter one another from the breeze. In hot dry or desert regions, on the other hand, the orientation of the building to minimise the exposure of external wall surface to the sun is paramount. Thus an orientation for inhabited spaces as near north/south as possible is important, as is the reduction to the minimum of those surfaces facing east and west which cannot be shaded from low altitude sunlight and which should have as few openings in them as possible.

As can so often be seen in vernacular buildings in desert regions, thick walls, small shaded openings, courtyards and protection from glare result in forms

entirely different from the more open configurations of Central Africa or South East Asia where air movement is at a premium.

Contrasting examples

A characteristic mid-twentieth century form that expresses the relationship between ward accommodation and the supporting departments in an extremely direct way is the multi-storey ward block rising above a spreading base of specialist accommodation. Simple and compact, the structure is fairly economical; it lends itself well to the vertical stacking of communications and services and can occupy relatively little space on the site. Such an arrangement, or a similar tall ward block with supporting departments in an adjacent wing, may sometimes be the only practicable type of solution where ground space is at a premium. However, if the building is of any considerable height and cannot reasonably be served by stairs or ramps in an emergency it relies entirely on an adequate lift installation for its efficient functioning.

The ward block may be naturally ventilated if it is narrow enough, as may be the base if it spreads widely around courtyards. But if the former is compactly planned, with beds around the perimeter and a central core of service rooms and communications, as is often the case, and the base is similarly condensed (implying full air conditioning) the building is almost totally dependent on its its mechanical equipment. It shares many characteristics with the international hotel building type but it may be doubted whether the functions a hospital has to fulfil are similar. Further, it tends to be a form that cannot readily be altered or extended in any organic manner.

In some developing countries, and particularly the oil-rich ones where air conditioning of major new buildings is taken for granted, this compact multi-storey arrangement, imported from elsewhere, could almost be said to have become a stereotype.

In the UK the image of the huge impersonal medical machine that this type of building all too easily presents has tended to become increasingly unacceptable to the public, and particularly to the potential patients. For this reason, quite independently of the economic consequence of running such a building and its longer term energy implications, the pendulum of preference has for some time been swinging strongly away towards a search for simpler technical methods, a more humane and domestic character, and more flexible solutions.

In some other countries, on the other hand, where health care is an emerging social facility, the imposing symbolism of a big building, and preferably a tall one,

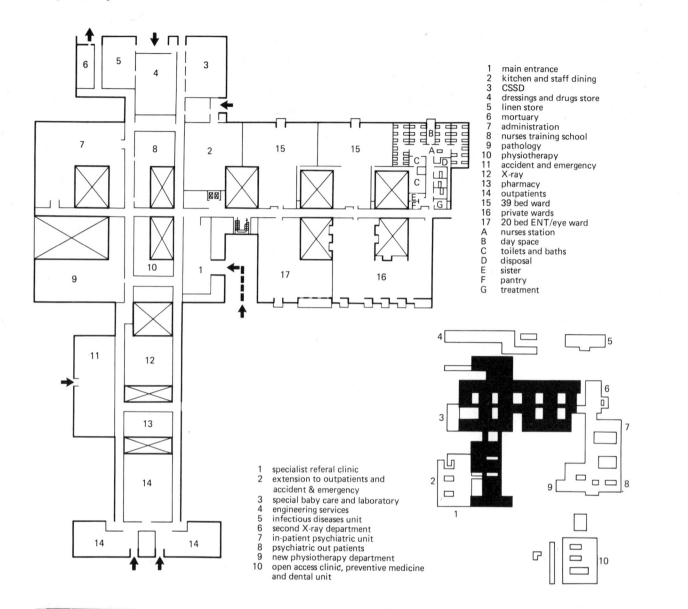

1 main entrance
2 kitchen and staff dining
3 CSSD
4 dressings and drugs store
5 linen store
6 mortuary
7 administration
8 nurses training school
9 pathology
10 physiotherapy
11 accident and emergency
12 X-ray
13 pharmacy
14 outpatients
15 39 bed ward
16 private wards
17 20 bed ENT/eye ward
A nurses station
B day space
C toilets and baths
D disposal
E sister
F pantry
G treatment

1 specialist referal clinic
2 extension to outpatients and
  accident & emergency
3 special baby care and laboratory
4 engineering services
5 infectious diseases unit
6 second X-ray department
7 in-patient psychiatric unit
8 psychiatric out patients
9 new physiotherapy department
10 open access clinic, preventive medicine
   and dental unit

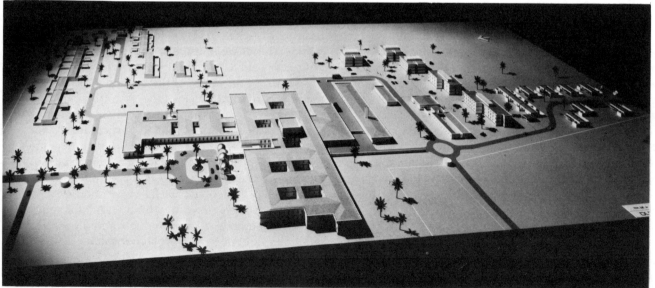

(facing page, top)
Ground floor of the Rashid Hospital, Dubai; a fully air-conditioned building with 393 beds. It has a simple and direct organisation of hospital streets relieved by internal courtyards. Men's wards are on the ground floor, women and children's on the upper together with the operating department and ITU, which adjoins the central lifts. Architect: John R. Harris

Extensions to the Rashid Hospital (shown in outline) add more beds, further diagnostic and treatment accommodation, a psychiatric unit and an open access outpatient clinic

(facing page, below)
Model of the Rashid Hospital. Outpatients, accidents, pharmacy and X-ray are in the single storey wing on the left; stores, CSSD and kitchen entrance on the right. (Photo: Henk Snoek Photography & Associates)

(above)
The Rashid Hospital, Dubai; air conditioned, with small window openings and balconies for the recessed day spaces in the wards. Kitchen, stores, CSSd and mortuary are in the unit on the right; outpatients, accident and emergency and X-ray are in the complementary wing on the other side of the main building. Architect: John R. Harris

(below)
Model for a 400 bed hospital on an urban island site in Khartoum, a hot dry climate. Outpatient, maternity, operating, diagnostic and service departments are at ground floor level, penetrated by small courtyards and air-conditioned only where medical needs justify it. Above this base there are four wards to each floor, facing north and south, deeply shaded and naturally ventilated, approached from a visitors' concourse served by ramp and lifts. In the foreground (right) there are shaded waiting and car parking areas. Architects: Architects' Co-partnership

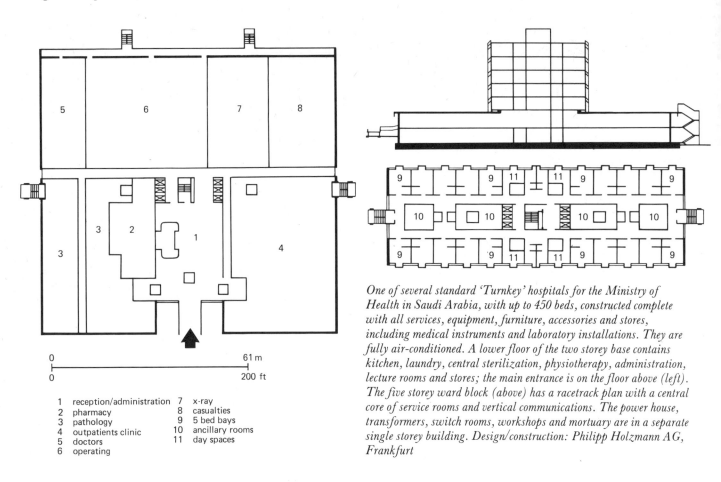

1 reception/administration
2 pharmacy
3 pathology
4 outpatients clinic
5 doctors
6 operating
7 x-ray
8 casualties
9 5 bed bays
10 ancillary rooms
11 day spaces

One of several standard 'Turnkey' hospitals for the Ministry of Health in Saudi Arabia, with up to 450 beds, constructed complete with all services, equipment, furniture, accessories and stores, including medical instruments and laboratory installations. They are fully air-conditioned. A lower floor of the two storey base contains kitchen, laundry, central sterilization, physiotherapy, administration, lecture rooms and stores; the main entrance is on the floor above (left). The five storey ward block (above) has a racetrack plan with a central core of service rooms and vertical communications. The power house, transformers, switch rooms, workshops and mortuary are in a separate single storey building. Design/construction: Philipp Holzmann AG, Frankfurt

One of the standard 'Turnkey' hospitals in Saudi Arabia

seems to catch the imagination of those politically responsible for its provision, even though there may be ample ground space for other types of solution. Whether it is a form really suitable for the culture and the technological resources of some areas of the world is highly questionable.

A relatively early British example of the opposite approach from the multi-storey ward block with the low base (or the matchbox on a muffin, as it has been called) can be seen at Wexham Park, Buckinghamshire, which was built during the first half of the 1960s. Here the multi-storey block contains only administration, secretarial services and residential accommodation for medical staff, none of whom are entirely dependent upon lifts but are only inconvenienced if they fail.

The wards, which provide about 300 beds, and the diagnostic, treatment and other servicing departments, are all of only one storey in height and are spread out in fingers around the taller block, enclosing courtyards and gardens of domestic scale. The hospital occupies a relatively large site area and from the point of view of journey times from one part of the building to another probably stretches to near the limit of acceptability a horizontal layout of one storey.

These two ways of solving the problem of the physical form of the hospital epitomise two fundamentally different approaches. One results in a sophisticated instrument, dependent on its supporting machinery, and is highly efficient provided the machinery works continuously. The other, although it may need more space, may be just as satisfactory clinically and although aided by machinery in certain parts, the function of the building is not entirely dependent upon it.

The simpler and non-mechanical solution may also offer a psychological advantage for staff and patients, particularly for patients who suddenly find themselves in an alien and disturbing world of medical procedures and unnatural intervention. Patients may obtain reassurance and perhaps a quicker recovery through relationships and symbols with which they can connect and which have some associations with their habitual lifestyle. To be fairly close to the ground, to open a window, to smell the world outside and hear its sounds may reassure the patient that he is still connected with the outside world. There is no straightforward answer to the question of which approach is the better.

Superb multi-storey hospitals of the mechanically

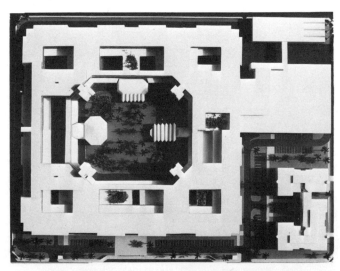

Model of Al-Karama hospital, Baghdad, a 1000 bed air-conditioned building on an island site. The hospital street runs round four sides of the central courtyard, with lifts and stairs at the corners, where the L-shaped wards are approached. There are two floors of wards, separated from the ground floor accommodation by an interstitial space for the distribution of services. On the ground floor of the rectangle are the specialist referral clinics, diagnostic and accident and emergency departments, education and administration. In the central courtyard are (left) the lecture theatre, (centre) the senior staff dining room and (right) the on-call suite. The wings on the right contain the operating theatres, sterilizing centre, supplies and laundry, with ramps connecting all floors. Staff residences are in the separate building. Architects: Architects' Co-Partnership

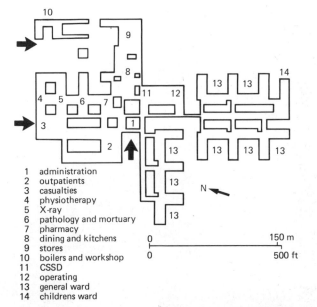

1 administration
2 outpatients
3 casualties
4 physiotherapy
5 X-ray
6 pathology and mortuary
7 pharmacy
8 dining and kitchens
9 stores
10 boilers and workshop
11 CSSD
12 operating
13 general ward
14 childrens ward

Wexham Park Hospital. Single storey wards extend in fingers to the south and west from the sterilizing and operating departments at the centre. Outpatients, pharmacy, casualties, X-ray and diagnostic departments extend at ground level around courtyards to the north; dining rooms, kitchen and stores to the east. Over the centre a higher building houses essentially non-clinical uses – administration and residential accommodation for medical staff. Architects: Powell and Moya

Wexham Park. The central administrative and residential building rises above the spreading single storey hospital. (Photo: Colin Westwood)

The two arms of each ward unit at Wexham Park enclose a sheltered garden. (Photo: Colin Westwood)

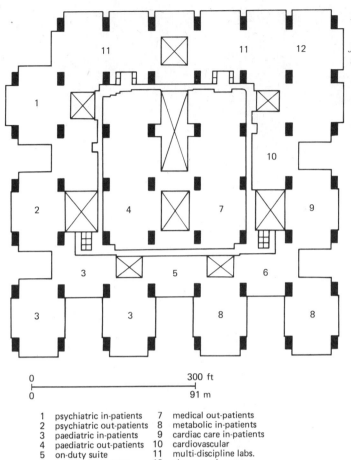

Diagram of the arrangement of one of the upper floors at McMaster. Vertical towers house either services or stairs and support the trussed floors. A continuous hospital street binds the assembly together and is lit at intervals from courtyards

| 0 | | 300 ft |
| 0 | | 91 m |

1	psychiatric in-patients	7	medical out-patients
2	psychiatric out-patients	8	metabolic in-patients
3	paediatric in-patients	9	cardiac care in-patients
4	paediatric out-patients	10	cardiovascular
5	on-duty suite	11	multi-discipline labs.
6	medical in-patients	12	electron microscopy

The Health Service Centre under construction at McMaster University, Hamilton, Ontario. A large and sophisticated complex embracing hospital, medical school, school of nursing, and research, it aims to provide a simple envelope within which integration of departments, highly developed services and opportunities for change are possible. Mechanical services are distributed to the usable floors through the long-span spaces between the deep trusses, fed from service towers arranged on a rectangular grid. Architects: The Zeidler Partnership

*The McMaster hospital street where it passes alongside one of the
courtyards*

dependent type have been built during recent decades, notably in the USA and Canada. Here the complexity of distributing services such as conveyors, liquids, gases and air, and maintaining these without conflicting with clinical work or putting it at risk, has prompted designs of great sophistication. The accommodation is supported by an armature of service zones which occupies almost as much space as the area it serves.

Instead of being stacked directly one upon another clinical and research floors have been separated like a sandwich by independent interstitial spaces high enough for maintenance engineers to walk about in, in which services can be distributed to any part of the floor area. These spaces have been fed vertically by major communication ducts or towers, thus separating entirely the servicing zones from those which are dependent upon them.

The advantages of configurations of this sort are not limited to the ease of maintenance they confer on the hospital when it is in use or has to be altered. By providing separate territories in which construction workers and service engineers can operate independently and simultaneously these structures simplify and accelerate the process of building and commissioning. At a strategic level they also provide a carcase within which considerable flexibility of internal planning is possible, as the need to group heavily serviced areas together, or to superimpose them floor by floor to simplify the routes of services, is largely eliminated.

Thus for the most complicated and sophisticated buildings, such as large teaching hospitals in which clinical and research facilities may need to be integrated, there may be good arguments to recommend them. However, although such arrangements may be lucid they are costly to build, and they are probably out of scale with the needs of the general hospital in many countries.

Growth and change

Some of the apparently rational and coherent hospital forms adopted by designers display more abstract architectural logic than sense of historical reality. They tend towards a finite notion of a hospital building, for implicit in them is the assumption that the operational policies and the balance of the various types of accommodation will continue relatively unchanged during the life of the structure.

This assumption is not always well founded. One has only to look at some of the older hospitals in Britain to recognise the extensions to the earlier core that have come about over the last century. These are usually without any strategic planning armature to hold them together but have been added largely *ad hoc* as new needs and opportunities have presented themselves.

There seems little reason to suppose that medicine will cease to produce unforseen demands and it is arguable that new hospitals will be subject to similar pressures. This is particularly so in developing countries where, although the initial accommodation may have to be relatively simple, the provision of facilities is likely to be rapidly extended in the future.

As the inevitability of growth and change has come to be recognised views have been expressed during the last few decades which maintain that, wherever it is situated, a hospital is never likely to be complete. As the building will inevitably require alterations and additions during its working life, from the outset its physical organisation should be conceived with this in mind.

The classic demonstration of this as a generating approach to planning is to be seen in the UK at Northwick Park, a district general hospital and clinical research centre, designed early in the 1960s. It is probably the most uncompromising and theoretically 'pure' evidence of this philosophy, and remains a seminal example that in one form or another has probably had as profound an influence as any on hospital planning strategy ever since.

Fundamental to the 'indeterminate' approach of Northwick Park is the concept of a linear and enclosed hospital street which provides a strategic backbone. Independent buildings for various functions can be attached to this with relative freedom, each building having one end connected to the street and the other unobstructed so that it can be extended laterally at some future date if this is necessary.

Although it is much more flexible, and at a higher level of sophistication, the basic pattern has similarities with the early military hutted hospital of the Crimean War, the old 'Fever hospitals' or the long 'Nightingale' wards. All of these (no doubt for quite different reasons) were characterised by accommodation placed at intervals and at right angles to a main access corridor or walkway.

With a planning strategy such as this the initial design, construction and commissioning of the building by stages is greatly facilitated. This is because the units are physically independent and not closely integrated with one another in a way that causes a change in one to have a ripple effect in contiguous departments. In addition, the growth of different parts is likely to be possible in large or small increments without interfering with others, as also is internal alteration to any individual part.

At Northwick Park no attempt is made to construct a finite architectural object. The indeterminacy is

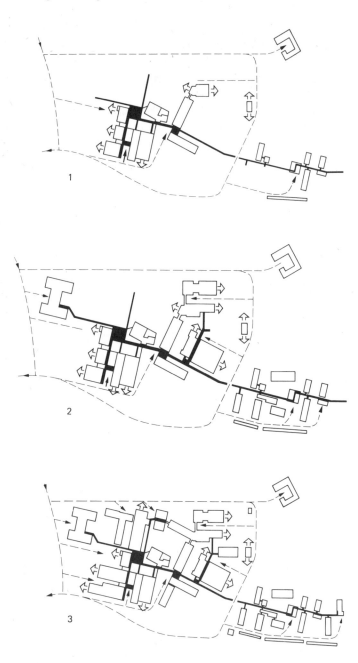

Northwick Park. The hospital street is on the right, used by patients, staff and visitors. Supply services occupy a separate street underneath. Dining rooms and lecture theatre are linked to the street on the left. In the background is a ward and research building. (Photo: Henk Snoek Photography & Associates)

Three plans showing the development method at Northwick Park Hospital and Clinical Research Centre. A linear hospital street forms the backbone to which ribs can be attached with relative freedom. It is the earliest example of deliberate indeterminacy in post-war hospital planning. Most of the hospital and research departments may be constructed, and later altered or expanded, independently of one another. Construction was carried out in phases over a period of nine years and during this time extensions and alterations to the original brief were made without disturbing the basic design. Architects: Llewelyn-Davies Weeks

pursued with a logic that permeates the whole design, almost to the extent of seeming to avoid any extraneous imposition of visual order except in the employment of dimensionally related components of construction. Indeed the total result might not unreasonably be likened to the loose appearance of the large nineteenth century hospital to which frequent extensions and annexes have been added in the surrounding grounds when they were needed. There is, however, the important difference, logistic rather than visual, that at Northwick each element adjoins a deliberate and predetermined pattern of communications and is arranged from the outset with the possibility of alteration and extension in mind.

The hospital street

The principle of a line of communication or 'hospital street' to which fingers or nodules of accommodation are attached can be seen in an elementary and more rigid form in a study for a 300 bed hospital at St. Albans in Hertfordshire, undertaken in the late 1940s. As at Northwick Park the hospital street was arranged on two levels, one for services and supplies and the other for all other purposes. This ran as a spine below a long ward block which was capable of horizontal growth by the addition of further ward units.

Diagnostic and treatment departments, extendable at their free ends, were plugged into the street at

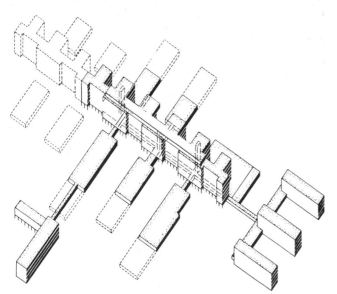

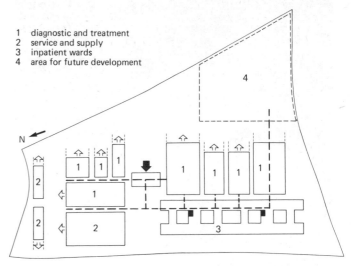

1 diagnostic and treatment
2 service and supply
3 inpatient wards
4 area for future development

A late 1940's study for a hospital in Hertfordshire. A two level hospital street for people and supplies runs below an extendable ward block, with vertical communication at intervals. Diagnostic and treatment departments and a separate maternity unit are plugged into the street, and are also extendable. Operating theatres are on the top floor. Architects: Architects' Co-Partnership

York District General Hospital. This provides 812 beds with the possibility of extension to over 1000. Most of the accommodation is between one and four storeys in height. Extendable diagnostic and treatment departments communicate at ground level with a simple linear hospital street for people and supplies which runs below a double-banked ward block that has cross links enclosing courtyards. Architects: Llewelyn-Davies Weeks

York District General Hospital

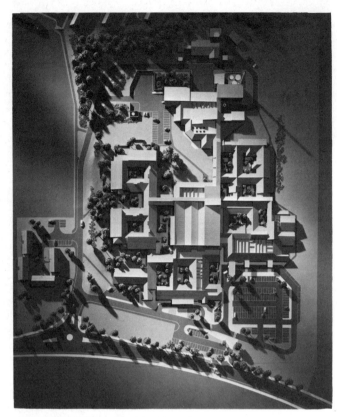

Model of the first stage of the North Tyneside District General hospital, providing 324 beds. The site falls from right to left of the picture and the buildings nowhere exceed two storeys. The operating and sterile supply departments are in the centre, linked on the left to a quadrangular ward building of two storeys. On the right they are linked to accident and emergency, intensive therapy and X-ray, which are single storey. The maternity department on the side nearest the main road is also single storey. Single storey childrens' wards adjoin, on the right, the spine that runs up to kitchen, dining room, stores and boiler house. The hospital streets incorporate ramps and stairs, and lifts are only necessary for transporting beds, trolleys, wheelchairs and heavy loads. Expansion to 600 beds is possible by the addition of further quadrangular ward blocks, day hospital, physiotherapy and outpatients to the right of the picture. Architects: George Trew Dunn Beckles Willson Bowes. (Photo: Henk Snoek/Crispin Boyle)

North Tyneside hospital is planned around intimate garden courtyards of varied scale and character. Services are distributed in enclosed and accessible routes within the pitched roofs. (Photo: Henk Snoek/ Crispin Boyle)

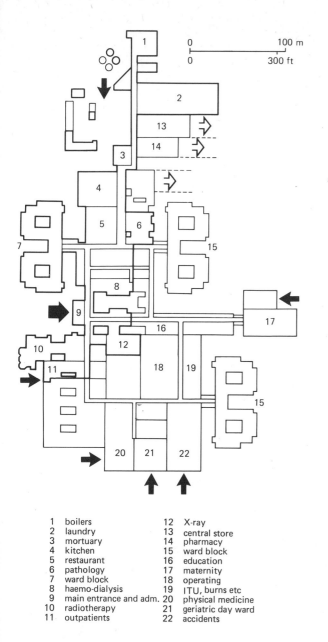

1	boilers	12	X-ray
2	laundry	13	central store
3	mortuary	14	pharmacy
4	kitchen	15	ward block
5	restaurant	16	education
6	pathology	17	maternity
7	ward block	18	operating
8	haemo-dialysis	19	ITU, burns etc
9	main entrance and adm.	20	physical medicine
10	radiotherapy	21	geriatric day ward
11	outpatients	22	accidents

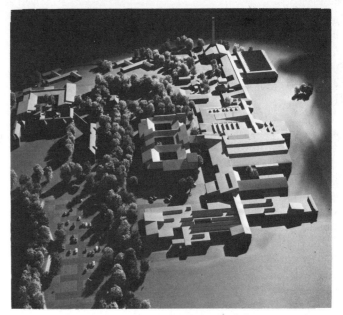

Model of the first stage of South Teeside hospital. Later stages enlarge the building by additions in the foreground and to the right of the picture. (Photo: Henk Snoek Photography & Associates)

South Teeside General Hospital. A low rise design similar to the North Tyneside example. Three storey quadrangular ward blocks of 360 beds are connected by short links to the central complex of supporting facilities, through which runs a rectangular system of hospital streets. Supply and service departments are attached to a linear tail. The first stage of construction (heavy outline) provides one ward block, haemo-dialysis, X-ray, radiotherapy, operating and a small out-patient department, in addition to boiler house, laundry, mortuary, kitchen and restaurant. Later stages add further ward blocks and a maternity unit, bringing the total number of beds up to about 1200, and enlarge the operating and outpatients departments and add intensive therapy, physical medicine, day wards, accidents, pathology, pharmacy and central stores. These enlargements can be made without interference to the completed stages and in most cases can be phased independently of the addition of ward blocks. Architects: George Trew Dunn Beckles Willson Bowes

ground level on the pattern of a fishbone. Much the same principle can be seen again in a later, larger and more developed form at the 800 bed York General Hospital, where the basic relationship of wards, hospital street and specialist departments is very similar.

The line of communication to which the various elements relate is not by any means invariably linear. It sometimes takes the form of either a loop, a figure of eight, a cross, or a combination of these patterns. In most hospitals it is not practicable, however desirable, to provide strict segregation between the streets for supplies or other goods and those for people, although by the disposition of departments it may be possible to avoid serious conflict between the major categories of

traffic, both from the point of view of its density and of the potential risk of cross-infection.

It is an advantage to avoid the routes for visitors being combined to any great extent with other internal circulation, for instance, and to arrange that potential traffic past critical areas such as operating suites is minimised. It is also desirable that infected and dirty material which is being removed for processing or disposal passes along routes which neither cross those constantly in use by patients and staff nor pass sensitive clinical areas. The latter include theatres and surgical wards, maternity departments, and places occupied by patients with reduced protection or immunity from infection.

The source of infection is not confined to clinical

areas. The origin of infection, and its results, can be in any part of a hospital including, for example, kitchens and laundries. Control of infection depends largely upon the behaviour and disciplines of people but it can be greatly assisted by the physical planning of the building.

The arrangement of the elements of accommodation along a linear hospital street can demand a lot of space on the site and in a large hospital may result in travel distances that are unacceptably extended. It can also be argued that, in some forms, this arrangement encourages the isolation of specialities in separate units and may create physical and psychological obstacles that inhibit intercommunication.

The tendency of individual medical disciplines to merge with one another or to become interdependent suggests the need for a form that provides close relationships. There is a conflict between integrated planning and patterns which are looser. The former tends to encourage the search for the perfect answer at a particular moment in history. The looser forms permit not only an ebb and flow beween disciplines but can also respond to pressures which it is difficult and sometimes impossible to anticipate.

A British sequence

An outline of four examples of the trend of design thinking in Britain as represented by the Ministry of Health (subsequently the Department of Health and Social Security) and the Regional Hospital Boards is given below. These demonstrate, over a period of years, a series of different types of solution to the problem of the general hospital in the context of a large, continuous and centrally financed national hospital building programme in which there has been development work, feedback and redevelopment, in parallel with an increasing need for economy. In addition to setting standards, controlling costs and publishing guidance notes the Ministry has sponsored research and design and development work, some of which it has carried out itself.

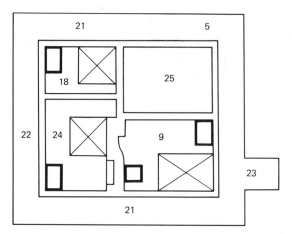

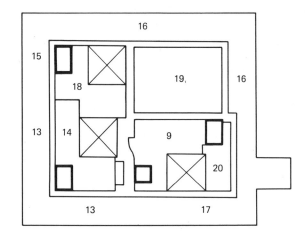

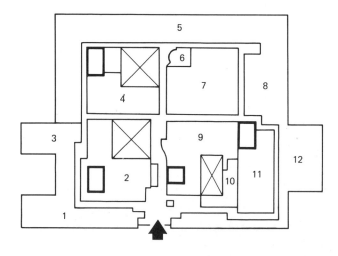

Diagrams of the general arrangement of the three principal floors of Greenwich District General hospital; 800 beds in a fully air-conditioned, compact, low-rise format. A rectangular hospital street surrounds the core of specialist departments, relieved by three courtyards. The clinical floors are separated by interstitial service floors, connected by four vertical shafts (heavy outline). The beds are banded continuously around the perimeter. Below the main entrance floor (bottom plan) a semi-basement contains principally food preparation for the three floor kitchens above, car parking and boiler house. Architect: W. E. Tatton Brown, Department of Health and Social Security, with the S. E. Metropolitan Regional Health Board

1	outpatients clinic	13	maternity wards
2	ante-natal	14	delivery/special care babies
3	day theatres and ward	15	gynaecological wards
4	geriatric day hospital	16	surgical wards
5	geriatric wards	17	orthopaedic wards
6	chapel	18	administration
7	x-ray	19	operating
8	psychiatric unit	20	intensive therapy
9	kitchen/dining	21	medical wards
10	dispensary	22	paediatric wards
11	accident & emergency	23	isolation
12	physical medicine	24	training centre
		25	pathology & mortuary

Greenwich

The first major example was the Greenwich District General hospital in South London which has 800 beds to serve a population of some 165 000. Built at about the same time as Northwick Park it exemplifies a very different approach. Greenwich was, of course, a response to a different problem, at a different scale and on a relatively urban site. Whilst it attempted to make provision for future change, to allow for growth was not part of its objective and it is thus considerably more compact.

Greenwich has three clinical floors, all 2.75 m clear height, superimposed in a simple rectangular shape and separated from one another by interstitial service floors. Instead of being linear, the hospital street is rectangular and within it are enclosed all the specialist departments except out-patients.

All wards are arranged on the perimeter of the building in a continuous band around the hospital street, separated from it by their ancillary rooms. Within the rectangle of the street the diagnostic, treatment and supply departments form the core of each floor, divided by corridors into four quarters. This core is perforated by three courtyards, as the building is not so high as to render relatively small courtyards unacceptable. The whole building is air-conditioned.

Although a large hospital, the form of the building facilitates rapid horizontal movement between departments which need to have close relationships. For example surgical beds, gynaecology, the maternity suite, theatres and intensive therapy are all grouped on the same floor. Vertical communication by lifts and the irritating waiting time that can result is cut to a minimum. In addition to lifts there is some interfloor communication by escalator, which in a low rise building is quick and easy for many purposes.

The opportunity for horizontal travel also facilitates the movement of bedfast patients in case of fire. They can readily be wheeled in their beds into a separate and remote fire compartment with little risk of having to be evacuated by stair or lift.

The location of the diagnostic and treatment departments in the central core of the building enables them to be planned where they are most convenient functionally. But, on the other hand, they cannot easily expand, for they are imprisoned on all four sides by the wards. The continuous peripheral banding of the wards offers opportunities for minor changes in the extent of one nursing unit at the expense of its neighbour without major alteration. However, this banding tends to make for relatively extended walking distances along straight corridors within each unit.

Although Greenwich was not designed with major expansion in mind it makes provision for alterations to

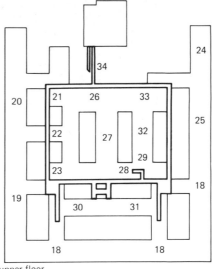

upper floor

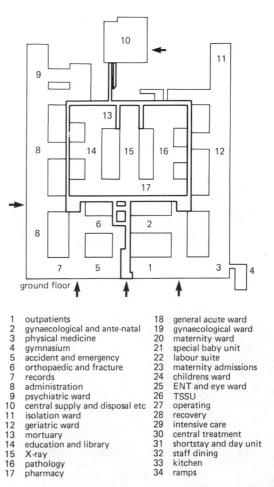

ground floor

1	outpatients	18	general acute ward
2	gynaecological and ante-natal	19	gynaecological ward
3	physical medicine	20	maternity ward
4	gymnasium	21	special baby unit
5	accident and emergency	22	labour suite
6	orthopaedic and fracture	23	maternity admissions
7	records	24	childrens ward
8	administration	25	ENT and eye ward
9	psychiatric ward	26	TSSU
10	central supply and disposal etc	27	operating
11	isolation ward	28	recovery
12	geriatric ward	29	intensive care
13	mortuary	30	central treatment
14	education and library	31	shortstay and day unit
15	X-ray	32	staff dining
16	pathology	33	kitchen
17	pharmacy	34	ramps

The 'Best Buy' hospital provides 550 beds on two storeys. The format has some similarity to Greenwich but the plan is perforated with courtyards, permitting a large measure of natural ventilation and lighting throughout the building. Beds occupy only three sides of the rectangle; on the fourth a separate works and supplies unit is linked to the hospital street by ramps.

its internal planning and servicing. Long spans of 19.5 m leave the floors relatively unencumbered by structural columns or walls. The clinical floors are separated by interstitial spaces for the distribution, maintenance and alteration of services (whose 1.7 m height is probably less generous than desirable).

But in spite of its potential internal flexibility, and although it was in fact constructed in stages, it is fundamentally a finite solution. In some respects the building is easier to extend than a tower and podium but, nevertheless, this type of arrangement does not lend itself naturally to being built in instalments nor to organic growth beyond its original form.

With its interstitial spaces and the dependence on air-conditioning the building is relatively costly and, irrespective of merit, is unlikely to be applicable where economy is an overriding restraint. This has indeed proved to be the case. It is in its characteristically horizontal rather than vertical deployment of space that its approach is most obviously echoed in later general hospital design in Britain.

Best Buy

This simpler and less costly solution was initiated by the Ministry of Health in the 1960s and has subsequently been further developed. In general conception it has affinities with Greenwich but is less solidly packed and relies almost entirely on natural light and ventilation.

The building is arranged on only two storeys and has no interstitial service spaces. Because of its economy (some of which was sought by omitting departments customarily found in District General Hospitals, such as central sterilisation and laundry, that could reasonably be shared with other hospitals in the vicinity) the design was called 'Best Buy' – a persuasive title that is indicative of the desire of a central government department to encourage semi-autonomous outlying executive authorities to adopt its suggestions.

The 'Best Buy' hospitals at Frimley, in Surrey, and Bury St. Edmonds, Suffolk, are smaller than Greenwich, each providing about 550 beds. Although in essence they have the same rectangular hospital street enclosing the central diagnostic and treatment departments they are less compact and are lit and ventilated by internal courtyards, as if fresh air had been injected into the solid form of Greenwich.

The accomodation around three sides of the perimeter is mostly wards, approached from three lengths of the rectangular hospital street, from which it is separated by further courtyards. On the fourth side of the rectangle an independent works and supply unit, from which material can be moved by trains of tugs pulling trolleys, is connected by ramps to both floors of the street.

Air view of the 'Best Buy' hospital at Frimley Park, Surrey.
Architects: Hospital Design Partnership, with the DHSS Hospital
Design Unit. (Photo: Handford Photography, by courtesy of
Holland, Hannen & Cubitts Ltd)

Harness

Both Greenwich and 'Best Buy' were in a sense model
hospitals. They were based on a ring of circulation
and conceived as a whole. They offered little opportunity for future growth, or for construction and
taking into use by stages.

The development that followed, known as
'Harness', was conceived in terms of a more open-
ended aggregation of units of accommodation along a
linear spine of circulation. It may be regarded not only
as a system of hospital planning but also as an
administrative method. 'Harness' attempted to em-
body the results of research and experience in the
formulation both of standardised plans for the various
departments, and of a method by which these could be
fitted together in a variety of ways. This was done in
anticipation that there would be an acceleration of
hospital building in the 1970s which would inevitably
involve many designers and 'clients' who were inex-
perienced in the overall complexities of hospital
planning. Whilst 'Harness' offered scope for different
arrangements, not the least of its objectives was to
reduce the lengthy process of individual design and to
simplify questions of functional acceptability and the
control of building cost.

'Harness' was intended for general hospitals of from
600 to 1100 beds. It was based on standard operational policies, for which plans for units of accommodation
for most of the departments were designed. The units
were of different sizes but dimensionally related to a
15 m clear span square grid. These units were capable
of arrangement in a variety of combinations and of
superimposition up to a height of four storeys,
'harnessed' together by a linear hospital street from
which further spurs of communication could run at a
right angle. The resulting assembly produced a
pattern of accommodation enclosing courtyards which

provided natural light and ventilation to the perimeter
of all the units.

The conception extended beyond unit plans for the
various departments. It was combined with a standardised precast structural system with which the units
could be constructed. Natural ventilation virtually

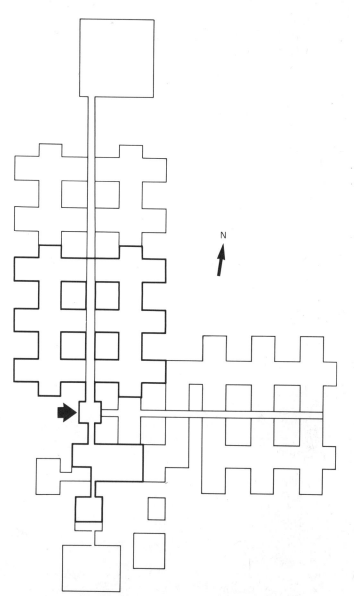

*Plan showing the first stage (heavy outline) and subsequent stages of
Maidstone District General Hospital, a two storey 'Nucleus'
arrangement. Wards, operating, accidents, x-ray, pharmacy, rehabilitation and administration are in the northern clusters; on the
southerly extension to the hospital street are the main entrance and
education, then pathology, mortuary, medical records, stores and
sterile supplies, and lastly the boiler house. Plant rooms rise above the
general level of the roofs at the intersections with the hospital street.
The first stage provides 300 beds and later extensions northwards and
eastwards can increase this to 800, including accommodation for
geriatric patients and radiotherapy to the north and psychiatric day
patients to the east. Architects: Powell, Moya and Partners*

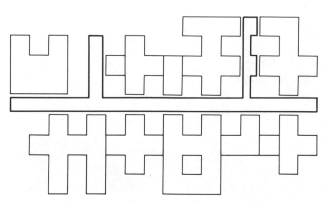

*The basic 'Harness' concept is a linear hospital street to which
standard and non-standard units of accommodation with different
configurations, planned on a 15 m square grid, are attached with
relative freedom but geometric consistency and enclose courtyards that
provide natural light and ventilation*

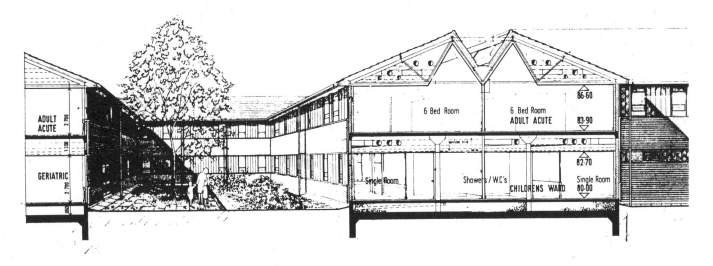

Sectional perspective of part of the 'Nucleus' District General Hospital at Maidstone, Kent, showing roof lighting and the distribution of services. Architects: Powell, Moya and Partners

Model of the first stage of Maidstone District General Hospital. (Photo: Sydney W. Newbery)

eliminated the need for large air-handling ducts. Unlike the relatively costly self-contained interstitial service zones of Greenwich, services were distributed from the hospital street within the structural spans, threaded through lattice beams and accessible from the ceiling of the floor below.

Nucleus

A neater and geometrically more lucid system of planning known as 'Nucleus' was developed from 'Harness'. It was conceived so that it offered the opportunity of the construction of a hospital in stages from a first phase of about 300 beds with the potential of expansion to about 900. The system could also be used for extending existing hospitals by the addition of various combinations of individual units. Like 'Harness' it is based on standardised operational policies and the aggregation of preplanned units along a linear hospital street, but it differs from 'Harness' in that each unit is a star shaped cluster or 'nucleus' of identical overall dimensions.

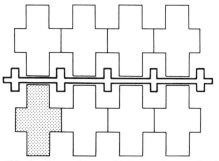

The basic 'Nucleus' is a cluster which contains wards, departments, or combinations of smaller departments. Placed side by side and connected to a linear hospital street the clusters produce a chequerboard of squares. All vertical circulation is related to the street

When set beside one another nucleus units produce a consistent geometry that results in a true chequer board of squares on a 16.2 m grid. The system is intended for buildings of a maximum of three storeys but preferably two, with natural lighting and ventilation to the majority of the accommodation.

Each cruciform element or cluster contains either wards or supporting departments. Typical accommodation within any one cluster comprises a pair of adult acute wards with a total of 56 beds; childrens' wards of 36 beds; operating theatres and post-operative recovery; accident and emergency and fracture clinic; adult day care, intensive therapy unit and central treatment; X-Ray and administration; out-patients, medical records and dispensary; rehabilitation, pharmacy, snack bar and staff change.

The 'industrial' accommodation for catering, stores, boiler house and works is not necessarily standardised but designed for the specific requirements of the

particular hospital and linked to the hospital street at an appropriate point.

Unlike its predecessor, 'Nucleus' is not integrated with a specific structural system. It provides a zoning strategy for the distribution of services from the hospital street and from roof plant rooms. The basic dimensions of the clusters permit a variety of methods of construction, a choice of materials and differences of architectural treatment. The system provides the potential for a low-key, domestic and humane atmosphere, the antithesis of the monumental and intimidating, particularly where it is restricted largely to two storeys.

Although producing a pattern that occupies a relatively large site area 'Nucleus' is not so demanding of space as the independent pavilion type of development along a linear street. It also offers better opportunities for the contiguity of departments. At the junction of one 'nucleus' with another this advantage is combined with a natural form of fire compartmentation and the opportunity of escape from one compartment into another.

Whilst placing restrictions on the potential growth of an individual department, unless it be at the expense of its neighbour or by the addition of a further nucleus or part of nucleus at the periphery, it is in principle a remarkably flexible approach. It gives the opportunity for the superimposition of various combinations of accommodation upon one another and for the addition of wards or servicing departments in two directions along extensions of the hospital street or along other streets developed at right angles to it.

The rationalisation of all ward units and various combinations of supporting departments into cruciforms of precisely the same dimension may perhaps be regarded with some degree of scepticism. This is particularly the case when the area of the cruciform has been reduced to a minimum. The horizontal travel distances that are likely to be involved in larger hospitals can also be questioned, especially if such distances are aggravated by economies that result in an inadequate provision of lifts.

Nevertheless it is a simple and ingenious arrangement and in sensitive hands is likely to result in buildings with a refreshingly human scale. In addition it is an approach that offers substantial advantages as a flexible strategy for development in phases, and for the rapid planning and implementation of a programme of new hospitals or of extending old ones. Encapsulating in a variable but readily usable form much previous experience of functional performance and operational economy 'Nucleus' provides a basic discipline that should eliminate much of the time so often spent in argument, briefing and the search for perfection and unique solutions.

Chapter 4
Wards

In-patient wards are classified by their speciality. In the General Hospital the usual ones are:
- the adult general acute
- the adult surgical
- the children's or paediatric
- the old people's or geriatric
- the maternity
- the orthopaedic
- the psychiatric.

Sometimes there are isolation wards for patients carrying an infection or who for some reason have suppressed immunity and need to be nursed in a bacteria-free environment. Adult wards are also likely to be differentiated by sex, depending on the way in which they are planned and the customs of the country.

Number of beds

Over a hundred years ago Florence Nightingale held that thirty-two was the maximum desirable number of patients in a ward unit. Although there have been revolutionary developments in medicine and surgery since then, and many changes in the way the ward has been planned, the number of patients that can be cared for by the ward sister and her team has remained remarkably similar.

Today the preferred number of patients in the general acute and surgical wards may be some four beds less than Florence Nightingale's thirty-two but it seems to be universally recognised that one team should not deal with more. Medical and surgical skill, centralised supplies and specialist facilities have not extended the range of what is sometimes known as 'tender loving care.'

The number of beds under one sister is likely to vary from about 28 to 30 in general wards, or about 20 to 24 for children. These numbers may be affected by nursing team arrangements, but in the interests of

flexibility and possible future changes, and also for structural and servicing reasons (particularly in multi-storey buildings) ward units are usually about the same overall size, varying only in their internal planning. Wards with fewer beds tend to be those needing additional ancillary accommodation particular to their speciality and the sizes even out reasonably.

Location

The location of wards in relation to other departments of the hospital is rarely critical, except that surgical wards and those for intensive care are best in close proximity to the operating theatres. It is an advantage if this connection does not depend on the use of lifts, although this cannot always be achieved.

However, all wards need to be easily accessible from the hospital's main supply and disposal routes and to have convenient communication with the diagnostic and treatment departments, particularly such departments as physiotherapy which are visited by ambulant in-patients. In addition all wards should be capable of being reached by visitors along simple and coherent routes from which they are unlikely to stray into other parts of the building from which they should be excluded, or to pass sensitive area where there are high risks of cross infection.

If the ward is to provide a sense of repose and be protected from excessive distractions and extraneous traffic it is important that it should be separated from the hospital's main communication routes. However, some modification of this may be desirable for the geriatric wards, where patients are not necessarily ill in the accepted sense and like to 'see the world go by'. No ward should be used as the principal means of access to another. Even though it may not be entirely on a cul-de-sac, the entrance to every ward should be capable of strict control.

Accommodation

The ward combines clinical and housekeeping facilities with the psychologically important function of providing the patient with a reassuring home in which he can be encouraged and supported towards an early recovery. The housekeeping element used to represent a much larger part of the work of the ward staff than it does today. This is now much reduced by centralisation of the supply of food, linen, drugs and sterilised articles, so that the ward no longer carries large local stocks of linen, crockery and medicines.

Local sterilisation of syringes, bowls and surgical instruments for minor procedures is usually superseded by the central supply of these items in packaged form. This has altered the nature of the work of the ward staff and has reduced the ancillary accommodation which is needed as part of the unit.

Apart from bathing, washing, toilet facilities and day spaces for ambulant patients, the ancillaries in the general ward normally consist of:

a treatment room where surgical dressings can be attended to and minor operative procedures carried out with the minimum risk of cross-infection and without distressing other patients,
a clean utility room principally for the preparation of equipment used in the treatment room,
a dirty utility room for emptying and cleaning bedpans and urine bottles, cleaning other soiled items and disposing of materials such as dressings,
a pantry for the preparation of beverages and for washing and drying crockery,
a small equipment store,
one or more nurses' stations,
an office,
provision for the storage of patients' clothes,
a cleaner's base,
a disposal room.

The treatment room is sometimes placed between the clean and dirty utility rooms so that sterilised equipment from the Central Sterile Supply Department (CSSD) can be received and prepared in the clean utility, passed through a hatch into the treatment room, and after use passed through another hatch to the dirty utility, where it is washed before return to the CSSD.

In some hospitals the clinical facility of the treatment room has been removed from the ward unit and has been centralised. From the patients' point of view this has the disadvantage that by specialising treatment and taking it away from the familiar ward staff it becomes impersonalised. It also affects training, because the student nurses' opportunities for experience are much reduced.

Development of form

The classic Nightingale ward is long and narrow. It is approached from one end, lit and ventilated from both sides, and has two rows of beds arranged to face one another, their heads against the window walls. At one or both ends of the ward are the ancillary rooms and lavatories. The nurses' station from which the ward is controlled and the day space for patients who can get out of bed are islands in the central passage between the feet of the beds.

Florence Nightingale did not invent this form, for it is a plan with a long history and appears, in 13th century French religious foundations, as a nave of beds with an altar at one end. In its 19th century form Florence Nightingale gave it her seal of approval as

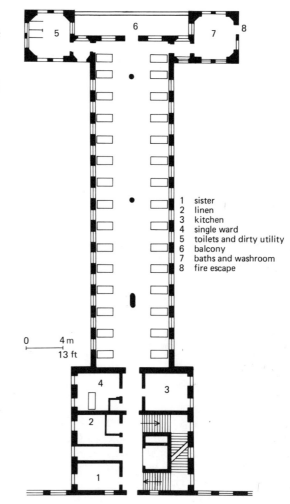

1 sister
2 linen
3 kitchen
4 single ward
5 toilets and dirty utility
6 balcony
7 baths and washroom
8 fire escape

0   4 m
13 ft

A 30-bed Nightingale ward at St Thomas' Hospital, London, little altered since it was built in 1871 except for the addition of some sanitary fittings and the substitution of radiators for the original open fires. The nurses' base is about half-way along the ward and the central isle beyond it is used as day space. The width of the ward is about 8 m and the length 35.5 m the recommended way of achieving cross-ventilation and nursing efficiency. Some of the wards at St. Thomas' hospital in London are an example from the 1870s and are still in use.

An interesting and remarkably successful cruciform variant from the end of the century, and also still in use, is to be found in another London hospital at University College. Here the long nave of the ward is

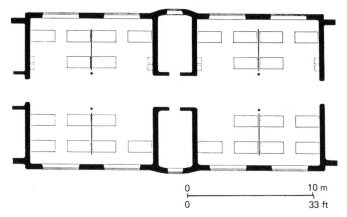

A ward at the Rigs hospital, Copenhagen, 1910. The width is 11.3 m. The freestanding screens at the bedheads were not full height. The enclosure at the centre accommodated a single bedded special care room and a nurse's room. Ancillary rooms were at the extremities

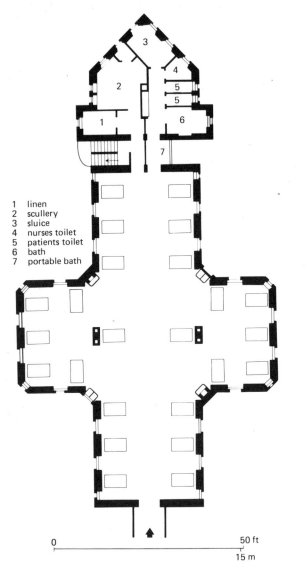

1 linen
2 scullery
3 sluice
4 nurses toilet
5 patients toilet
6 bath
7 portable bath

A variation on the Nightingale ward, built at University College Hospital, London at the beginning of the twentieth century. The width of the main 'nave' of the ward is about 7.6 m and the length 25.3 m. Sinks and washbasins were provided at the centre. It originally contained twenty-four beds but the capacity has subsequently been increased to twenty-eight by the addition of four beds backing on to short screen walls which spring from the central shafts and continue the line of the 'nave' at the crossing. The narrow access link has also been enlarged on both sides to form a ward pantry and linen room, and at the far end the bathrooms have been extended and the ward scullery converted into a treatment room

intersected by transepts that contain about a third of the beds and thus reduce its overall length. These transepts humanise its scale and provide some opportunity (whether or not it was originally intended) for the location of patients according to the nature or degree of the care they need.

An important change of direction in the planning of wards was introduced at the Rigs Hospital in Copenhagen in 1910. The 'nave' was wider and on both sides was subdivided by screens into bays. Each bay contained three or four beds arranged two deep and parallel to the external walls; patients no longer faced the light from the windows opposite.

Two such units of thirteen beds were set out symmetrically about a central nurses' room and a single bedded special care room, and other ancillary rooms and stairs were placed at the two extremities of the block. With the increasing desire for greater privacy than the Nightingale ward could offer this type of arrangement in multi-bed bays became common, although by no means universal, in the 1920s and 1930s. Sometimes the subdivision into bays was minimal, as at Rigs, but sometimes the bays were developed into partially or fully enclosed rooms, with various degrees of glazing to the central corridor. Except for a few single rooms the bays usually contained four beds.

In the USA the economics of personal health insurance arrangements led to three or two bed patterns with a higher degree of privacy from the corridor and influenced planning fundamentally. Elsewhere the larger multi-bed bay pattern combined with a proportion of single rooms has continued to find favour, with the important variation that beds are frequently planned three instead of two deep. This expedient shortens the walking distance along the adjacent corridor and is usually made acceptable for the beds furthest from the windows by the use of supplementary artificial lighting.

In the period immediately after 1945 hospitals in the UK and elsewhere were planned with bays of beds and ancillary rooms arranged on both sides of a central corridor, cross-ventilated naturally through the windows. Mechanical ventilation made possible the compression of this form into a double corridor plan in which the ancillary rooms occupied the centre of the building (lit and ventilated artificially) and the beds occupied the two external faces. This enabled the whole frontage of the block to be used for beds and shortened its length.

The logical development of this approach was what became known as the 'racetrack' or 'deep' plan. With this arrangement all four faces of the block were occupied by beds and dayrooms, served by a continuous 'racetrack' corridor which enclosed a central core of ancillary rooms and services. The precedent for

this came from North America, where on account of the extremes of climate and the acceptance of mechanisation, air-conditioning was regarded as a normal facility like drainage or electricity. Both 'racetrack' and double corridor plans have the advantage of concentrating the accommodation and reducing the length of journeys for the nursing staff. The ward units can be relatively compact instead of being strung out along corridors, and the external faces of the block can be occupied only by rooms which really need natural light and prospect.

In the early days of post-1945 hospital building there were some notable examples in the UK of this type of highly condensed ward plan. However, its virtues have not generally been thought to justify the high capital and running costs of the air-conditioning which it necessitates but which the climate does not always demand. There has consequently been little British development along these lines apart from exceptional cases, such as some of the major teaching hospitals or where buildings are situated in particularly polluted or noisy urban areas. Instead, the tendency has been towards solutions that place less reliance upon technology but still aim to achieve compactness.

Influences on form

A primary requirement for the planning of the ward unit is that its form should facilitate the care and attention given by the nursing team to the patients. Nurses are on their feet most of the time and the work is demanding and tiring. The number of journeys they have to undertake in the course of their spell of duty and the length of those journeys need to be reduced to a minimum if the care of the patients is to be maximised.

For this reason alone compactness is important; but it can also be valuable in helping patients to be aware of the nursing staff and not feel isolated. A compact form can facilitate easy communication between patients and nurses and make simple visual supervision practicable without recourse to elaborate and impersonal electrical aids. As many beds as possible should be capable of being observed not only from the nurses' station or 'staff base' but also by nurses as they go about the ward on their routine duties. In this way not only do the nursing staff know what is happening in the ward but patients are reassured by their presence. When strung out along a corridor the subdivision of the ward into multi-bed bays or separate rooms can tend to work against contact of this nature.

It must be said, however, that the importance of this involuntary contact between nursing staff and

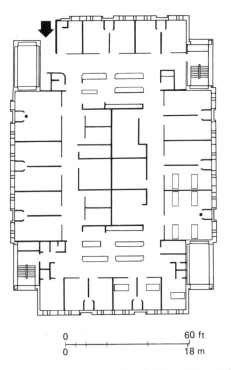

0 ————————— 60 ft
0 ————————— 18 m

A typical ward plan at the McMaster Health Science Centre, Hamilton, Ontario. The thirty-six beds are divided into two eighteen-bed units on a racetrack plan, each unit grouped around a nurses' station and work area that overlooks the single rooms for patients requiring intensive nursing care. The other bays are convertible into either two-bed or four-bed units. All rooms have immediate access to lavatories. The central core contains a treatment room, storage, offices and conference rooms, and a visitors waiting room. Architects: The Zeidler Partnership

patients seems to be a particularly British concern and is rarely much reflected in the planning of sophisticated wards elsewhere. Why this should be so is by no means clear. What does seem clear is that easy 'observability' simplifies the task of the nurses and should help a small team to give patients better attention than might otherwise be possible.

Probably the most significant influence on the design of wards was the Nuffield study on aspects of the hospital, begun in 1949 and published in 1955. Also, the experimental prototype wards that the Nuffield team built to test their conclusions. Their work on wards was based on a functional investigation of what the nursing methods were, what actually took place in the ward, the number of journeys undertaken daily and their length, the relative number of patients who were either bedfast or ambulant (or potentially ambulant) and the actual space necessary for the staff to perform certain functions without inconvenience.

Amongst other considerations the study examined the constraints and opportunities of daylight, sunlight, ventilation and acoustics. The method of approach was remarkably fresh at the time it was undertaken and the resulting publication was clearly expressed and easily understandable. Its influence on ward planning in the UK and elsewhere has been considerable. If, a quarter of a century later, some of its conclusions do not seem to be so inevitable many of the questions into which it attempted to probe need to be kept prominently in mind when designing wards today.

The traditional method of staffing a ward is to have one ward sister responsible for a team of nurses of various degrees of experience, some of them students, who are overseeing the welfare of some twenty-eight to thirty-two patients. But it is important to appreciate that the planning of the Nuffield prototype wards was based on the sister supervising two nursing teams,

each of which had about twenty patients in its care. Thus there were two nurses' stations instead of one. The size of the whole unit was bigger than normal, but each nursing team's knowledge of the people it was looking after was increased because it had fewer patients. There were also economies in the amount of ancillary accomodation needed because it could serve a larger number of patients than was determined by a ward unit of conventional size.

The Nuffield ward plans at Musgrave Park in Belfast, Northern Ireland, and Larkfield in Greenock, Scotland, which were designed in the early 1950s, reflect this organisational difference and demonstrate the importance of understanding operational policy as a basis for design. Conversely, they indicate how a pre-determined layout could dictate the nature of an operational policy.

Comparative examples

The wards of two general hospitals designed in the late 1950s, at Slough and at High Wycombe, about 30 miles from London, also demonstrate this bi-nuclear

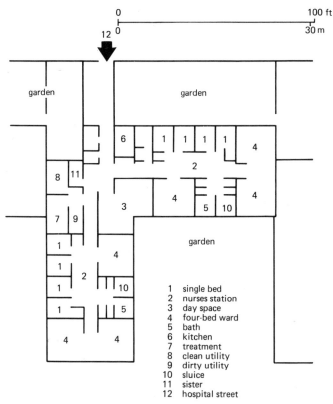

1 single bed
2 nurses station
3 day space
4 four-bed ward
5 bath
6 kitchen
7 treatment
8 clean utility
9 dirty utility
10 sluice
11 sister
12 hospital street

A 'bi-nuclear' ward in the single storey hospital at Wexham Park. Two sixteen-bed nursing units, each with its nursing station, are entered from the hospital street at the centre of gravity and not at one end as at Larkfield. All the bed spaces and the shared day space overlook small scale garden courts. Architects: Powell and Moya

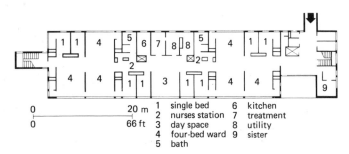

1 single bed
2 nurses station
3 day space
4 four-bed ward
5 bath
6 kitchen
7 treatment
8 utility
9 sister

The Nuffield experimental ward at Larkfield Hospital, Greenock; a 'bi-nuclear' arrangement in which two sixteen-bed nursing units, each with its own nursing station, share ancillary rooms and day space and are supervised by one sister. The bed bays and some of the single rooms have a lavatory immediately adjacent. The ward has natural cross-ventilation. Architects: Llewelyn-Davies Weeks

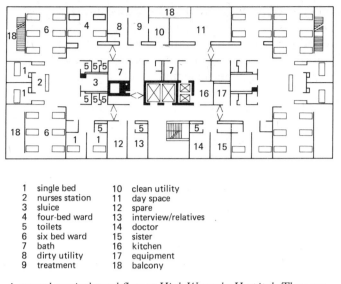

1 single bed	10 clean utility
2 nurses station	11 day space
3 sluice	12 spare
4 four-bed ward	13 interview/relatives
5 toilets	14 doctor
6 six bed ward	15 sister
7 bath	16 kitchen
8 dirty utility	17 equipment
9 treatment	18 balcony

A general surgical ward floor at High Wycombe Hospital. There are forty beds in two units, with two nurses' stations and one sister's room. The bed areas at each end are separated by doors from the central facilities. Each 20 bed unit is grouped around the nurses' working area and patients' lavatories. There is a notably good view of the beds from the nurses' station and across the building from one multi-bed bay to another. Architects: Powell and Moya

1 single bed	7 bath
2 nurses station and clean utility	8 dirty utility
3 ward office	9 pantry
4 treatment	10 equipment
5 toilets	11 day space
6 six bed ward	12 staff room

A ward layout for St Mary's Hospital, Paddington. There are four wards of twenty-eight beds, each closely grouped around a nurses' station and clean utility area, behind which are the other ancillary rooms. Day spaces intercommunicate between adjacent wards. The design aims to preserve some of the qualities of the Nightingale Ward while retaining the flexibility to nurse men and women in the same unit and to allocate beds according to the patient's dependence on nursing supervision. Architects: Llewelyn-Davies Weeks

The nurses' station at High Wycombe, looking towards a six bed bay. (Photo: Bill Toomey/Architects Journal)

subdivision into two areas of nursing responsibility. Both are based on two units of twenty beds; they contain identical accommodation but are arranged in very different ways. The Slough building follows the linear form of Larkfield. At High Wycombe the site was too restricted in exent and the wards were therefore planned in a more concentrated 'racetrack' form; it was the first hospital in Britain to adopt this format.

Soon after High Wycombe had been taken into use it became clear that it was functioning particularly well in terms of patient care. An evaluation and comparison of the two hospitals was undertaken to try to identify the extent to which its success might be attributable to design.

The most significant conclusion was the superiority of High Wycombe on account of the way in which the majority of beds were closely grouped in an almost semi-circular arrangement around the ends of the block, enclosing the working area and nurses' station. Subdivided into single rooms and relatively open multi-bed bays the beds were nevertheless easily observed from the nurses' station and there was a degree of visual contact between beds on opposite sides of the building.

The evaluation noted that in contrast to the linear form full use could be made of the available nursing staff, which was of great importance when nursing skills were scarce. Indeed some consultants, junior doctors and nursing staff felt that if staff was short they would prefer a Nightingale ward to the linear pattern.

High Wycombe possesses much of the physical unity and ease of visual communication that has been remarked upon as the virtue of the Nightingale ward, but it must be noted that it provides only twenty beds to each nursing unit. It is harder to achieve this close grouping when the beds approach thirty in number.

An arrangement that has some of the characteristics of High Wycombe but does not depend on a 'racetrack' plan can be seen in one of the layouts for the projected rebuilding of St. Mary's Hospital at Paddington. In this case four wards of twenty-eight beds are approached from a central vertical access lobby. Each ward contains four multi-bed bays of six beds and four single rooms grouped around one nurses' station which backs on to the ancillary rooms.

A ward plan that departs from the Nightingale, the linear and the racetrack formats can be seen in the 'Harness' layout. But in the 'Nucleus' design the form provides a closer relationship between beds and the nurses' station. In 'Nucleus' two ward units, each of twenty-eight beds, are placed back-to-back with a common approach from the hospital street. Most of the ancillary rooms are in the core (there is no treatment room because this facility is centralised).

This layout, although condensed, allows two of the single rooms and half the beds in the multi-bed bays to be grouped around the staff base and the hub of the nurses' working area. The core is ventilated artificially and the bed areas are naturally lit and ventilated from the windows and the roof.

The geometrical ultimate of the Nightingale ward in terms of observability, ease of internal access, contact between patients and nurses, and a sense of community is a circle. In this the nurses' station is at the centre and the beds are disposed inside the circumference. Whether the degree of communication this arrangement provides is more valuable than the sense of relative privacy it destroys is open to argument; it

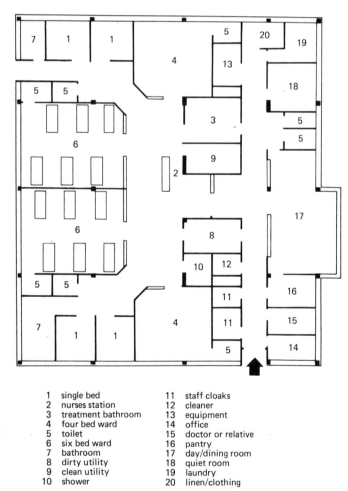

1	single bed	11	staff cloaks
2	nurses station	12	cleaner
3	treatment bathroom	13	equipment
4	four bed ward	14	office
5	toilet	15	doctor or relative
6	six bed ward	16	pantry
7	bathroom	17	day/dining room
8	dirty utility	18	quiet room
9	clean utility	19	laundry
10	shower	20	linen/clothing

A twenty-four bed geriatric ward unit with good visibility from the nurses' station, and with space around it for patients to be exercised and to practice mobility. Lavatories are within easy reach of all beds. Architect: R. G. Brown, North Western Regional Health Authority

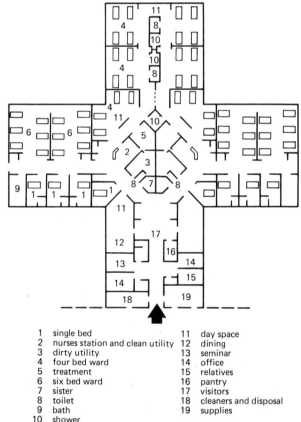

1	single bed	11	day space
2	nurses station and clean utility	12	dining
3	dirty utility	13	seminar
4	four bed ward	14	office
5	treatment	15	relatives
6	six bed ward	16	pantry
7	sister	17	visitors
8	toilet	18	cleaners and disposal
9	bath	19	supplies
10	shower		

A typical adult acute unit of 56 beds in the 'Harness' system. It comprises two wards of 28 beds, with their ancillary rooms planned back to back in the centre. The unit is approached from the hospital street through a shared corridor. The nurses' station and clean utility are at the centre of gravity of each ward, and in addition to the day/dining rooms smaller day spaces are distributed as part of the multi-bed bays. Architects: Department of Health and Social Security

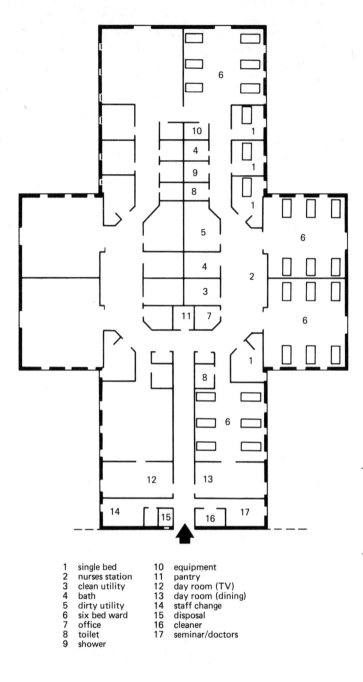

An adult acute bed unit of fifty-six beds in a 'Nucleus' cluster, comprising two wards of twenty-eight beds with back to back ancillary rooms in the centre, approached from the hospital street through a shared corridor. Progressive patient care can be practised within each ward, and the nurses' station has good observation, through glazed partitions, of two six bed bays and two single rooms (half the bed complement), an improvement upon the Harness arrangement. Architects: Hospital Design Partnership, with the Department of Health and Social Security

1	single bed	10	equipment
2	nurses station	11	pantry
3	clean utility	12	day room (TV)
4	bath	13	day room (dining)
5	dirty utility	14	staff change
6	six bed ward	15	disposal
7	office	16	cleaner
8	toilet	17	seminar/doctors
9	shower		

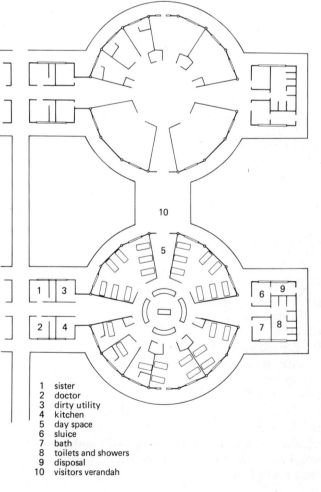

Two of a group of four single storey circular wards for a proposed hospital in Nigeria, approached from a hospital street and surrounded and linked by shaded verandahs. Each ward contains twenty-seven beds, three of them in single rooms with their own toilets. Other toilets, showers and the sluice rooms are in separate units. The nurses' station and clean utility is at the centre of the circle. Architects: Hospital Design Partnership

1	sister
2	doctor
3	dirty utility
4	kitchen
5	day space
6	sluice
7	bath
8	toilets and showers
9	disposal
10	visitors verandah

probably depends on the attitudes of the community for whom it is intended. Like many other things in hospital planning it is not a matter likely to be entirely susceptible to quantified evaluation and decision.

Early ambulation and progressive patient care

By no means all patients are confined to their beds all the time. In 1950 the Nuffield survey found that in a general surgical ward, a general medical ward and a gynaecological ward about half the patients were likely to be bedfast and about a quarter could get up to use a toilet and wash, perhaps with some assistance. The other patients were fully independent as far as their own toilet was concerned.

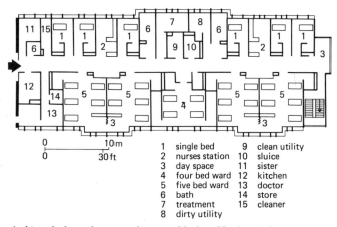

1	single bed	9	clean utility
2	nurses station	10	sluice
3	day space	11	sister
4	four bed ward	12	kitchen
5	five bed ward	13	doctor
6	bath	14	store
7	treatment	15	cleaner
8	dirty utility		

A thirty-bed ward in an eight storey block at Northwick Park. Although there are two nurses' stations the one nearest the entrance is the most generally used. All beds have toilets immediately adjacent and, in addition to the small room at the end of the block, day space forms a part of each five bed bay. These paired bays can be worked together or separated from one another if men and women occupy adjacent bays. Architects: Llewelyn-Davies Weeks

It was anticipated that under a more advanced regime of early ambulation only about a quarter of the patients would need to be actually confined to bed, and subsequent experience in Britain has confirmed that this is indeed the case. The implications of this on the provision and location of toilet accommodation and day room space in the ward, and on the journeys nurses need to make with bedpans and other equipment, are far reaching.

The encouragement of early ambulation has led to the dispersal of lavatories throughout the ward so that they are within easy reach of the beds, and in some hospitals to their provision immediately adjoining each multi-bed bay.

The concept of Progressive Patient Care, which in essence means that the patient receives a degree of care that is appropriate to the phase of his illness, can be applied at all levels of the health service as it is inseparable from the concept of primary, secondary and tertiary care. In some hospitals it has been developed towards something nearly analogous to a specialised production line in which the patient moves from one part of the establishment to another according to his degree of recovery. But if taken to its logical conclusion this approach is questionable, for it can create problems in maximising bed occupancy and destroy the continuity of nursing care by shifting the patient from one team to another. It can also be disturbing for the patient, particularly if his condition is not improving.

Progressive Patient Care, as it affects the accommodation in the general hospital, normally implies only two categories: the general medical, surgical or specialised wards, and the Intensive Therapy Unit or Intensive Care ward, an independent department.

A third category, at the opposite end of the spectrum from intensive care, might be 'self-care' accommodation, of which there are examples in some developing countries although it is not yet much found elsewhere. It may well be adopted more frequently in the future as the cost of conventional medical care, particularly its staffing, continues to rise so alarmingly.

Ambulant patients who do not need frequent clinical attention but who are nevertheless not ready for discharge might well leave the ward and look after themselves or be cared for by relatives in nearby hostel accommodation. This would leave the beds occupied only by patients whose condition merits supervision by expensive nursing staff.

Within the normal ward Progressive Patient Care has implications on its arrangement. These are partly in the location of the beds for patients who need the closest attention, which are usually placed near the nurses' station for ease of observation, and also in the facilities provided for patients as a consequence of the policy of early ambulation.

The location of toilet facilities has already been mentioned. There may also be two degrees of day room space, the first adjacent to the actual beds, where one bed is sometimes omitted from a multi-bed bay to give sitting space within immediate reach of the bed area, and the second by the provision of separate day spaces within the ward. The latter are of particular value for meals and as places where ambulant patients can meet one another and their visitors in a relatively domestic atmosphere. By this method some of the potential disruption that sociability can impose on the routines of the bedfast can be

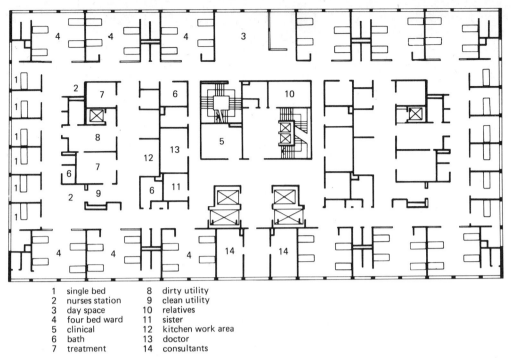

1	single bed	8	dirty utility
2	nurses station	9	clean utility
3	day space	10	relatives
4	four bed ward	11	sister
5	clinical	12	kitchen work area
6	bath	13	doctor
7	treatment	14	consultants

A typical ward floor at the West Middlesex Hospital. Two thirty-bed wards, each with a sister's room and two nurses' stations. Two thirds of the four-bed bays and two of the single rooms have lavatories adjoining. Day space is shared between the two wards. Architects: Robert Matthew, Johnson-Marshall & Partners

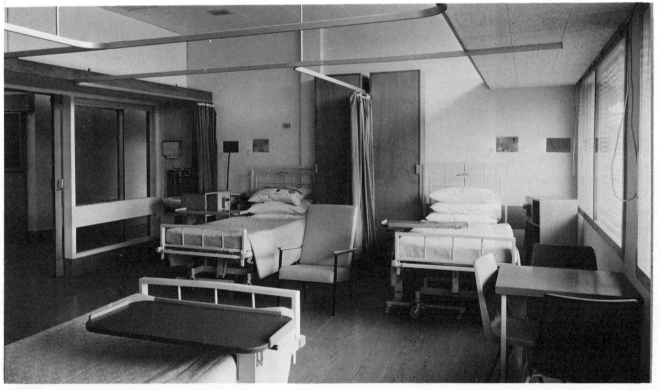

A four-bed bay at the West Middlesex, overlooked from the nurses' station. The corridor partition is fully glazed with sliding doors

avoided. These day spaces are often provided as two separate rooms, for quiet and noisy activities, and can sometimes be arranged at the interface between two ward units so that they can be shared.

Flexibility

If a hospital is to perform its function efficiently in the delivery of health care it is clear that it must aim to discharge is patients as soon as it is clinically satisfactory to do so. It must also operate with the minimum practicable number of empty beds. Two factors that conspire to hinder this are the relative number of patients needing admission to particular wards at any one time and the relative number of men and women within each category.

Although some hospitals have introduced ward units that accommodate both sexes, and in the case of psychiatric wards this is usually the practice, many wards are for one sex only. Thus in a hospital with wards that are too finite and geographically isolated from one another (for instance if each ward unit is on a separate floor of a multi-story building) there can be no common ground between one unit and the next into which it is possible for one of them to expand temporarily into its neighbour. If all the units are large Nightingale wards or of similar configuration, allocated to one sex only, beds may be left empty in one when there is unusual pressure on another.

For these reasons, contiguity of planning between one ward unit and another is an advantage, for it offers some measure of nursing flexibility between adjacent units. The breaking down of each unit into smaller bays or rooms can also provide some flexibility in the numbers admitted of each sex. Sometimes a few beds in single rooms occupy the interface between two wards; these are known as 'swing beds' and can be used by either ward according to need.

The peripheral forms of ward planning known as 'banding' may offer some degree of flexibility that might on occasions be useful. Examples of this are at Greenwich and in the most recent building at St. Thomas' hospital, London, or in a linear form at York, or even the Nucleus arrangement where two intercommunicating ward units are placed back to back. All provide some scope for variations in the relative numbers of men and women, not only by virtue of their subdivisions and a proportion of single rooms, but also by their relationship to their next door neighbour.

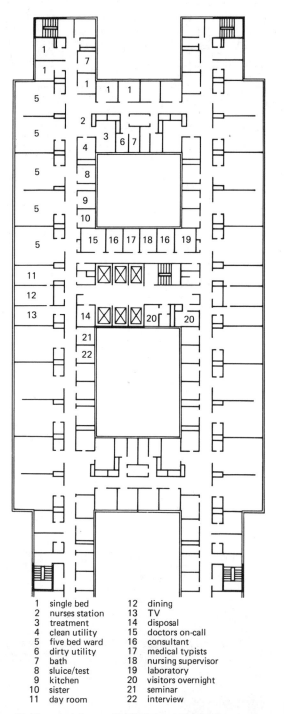

1	single bed	12	dining
2	nurses station	13	TV
3	treatment	14	disposal
4	clean utility	15	doctors on-call
5	five bed ward	16	consultant
6	dirty utility	17	medical typists
7	bath	18	nursing supervisor
8	sluice/test	19	laboratory
9	kitchen	20	visitors overnight
10	sister	21	seminar
11	day room	22	interview

Half a ward floor at York General Hospital, comprising four thirty-bed nursing units, each with one nurses' station. Each unit has five single rooms with five multi-bed bays of five beds; the single rooms in the cross links are 'swing beds' and may be used by either of the two flanking units as required. All multi-bed bays and two of the single rooms have their own lavatories. Day, dining and TV rooms are shared between adjacent units. The ward building is four storeys in height and is naturally ventilated. Architects: Llewelyn-Davies Weeks

Subdivision

Although the ward unit is now customarily subdivided into bays and single bedded rooms, opinions differ about the number of beds to a bay and the proportion that should be provided in separate rooms. Bays usually contain between four and six bed spaces and the beds are usually, but not necessarily, arranged parallel to a window wall. Six bedded bays make for compactness but have been criticised because the middle bed is an island and its occupant cannot avoid a neighbour whichever way he turns – a refinement that may not be of much significance for the average short-stay patient.

In the UK two and three bedded bays are generally regarded as unsatisfactory, principally on the grounds that two patients may prove to be mutually incompatible and that one of three may be the odd man out. But this view does not appear to be universally held in

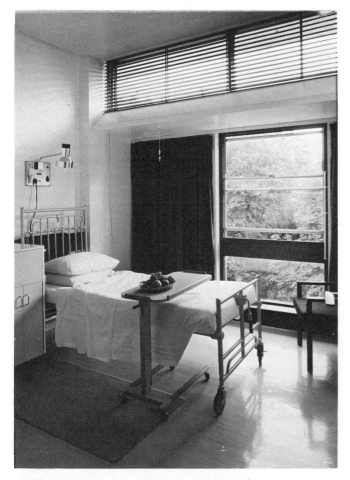

A single room in the ophthalmic department at the Royal Berkshire hospital, Reading. Glare from the sky is reduced by the overhang of the floor above and by the horizontal screen above eye level, which also helps to reduce the scale of the room. Architects: Architects' Co-Partnership

Europe, nor in the USA, where two bedded rooms, have for long been common, presumably as the nearest approach to the seclusion of single room that patients can afford under their Insurance arrangements.

Some single rooms are normally regarded as essential for clinical reasons. In the UK the usual number in a general acute ward of about thirty beds is a minimum of four, of which two have their own toilets *en suite* to ensure that the patient can be isolated and the risk of cross-infection by the transfer of bedpans to the dirty utility room is eliminated. It has been argued that more single rooms should be provided and that the greater their number the greater the flexibility and the fewer the beds that will be left empty because of sex or medical incompatibility. It has also been widely held that most patients dislike the open or semi-open ward and want privacy, and that the ideal is a hospital consisting entirely of single rooms.

Although the minority who can pay for the privilege of a private room seem to prefer to do so, from whatever motive, for the majority of patients the efficiency of the nursing is probably of more importance to their recovery than is privacy. It is clear that a relatively open arrangement is more conducive to good supervision and the satisfaction of the patients' needs by a limited staff than is a cellular pattern. If resources are to be used economically, single rooms should in the main be allocated only to those whose medical condition demands isolation, for instance to those who are a source of infection or are susceptible to it, or who are noisy or disruptive or otherwise disturb or distress other patients.

Privacy

Where a general hospital offers rooms for a minority of patients who pay for the privilege of privacy or of other advantages there may be the possibility of planning them in association with a pair of ward units. They can then share ward staff and some of the centralised ancillary rooms and can also be made available for public rather than private use in an emergency. Today such private accommodation usually has a bath and toilet *en suite* with the room, frequently placed on the corridor side.

In hot dry climates, where protection from the heat and glare is needed and only small windows are indicated, there is much to be said for locating the toilets on part of the room's external wall, and this arrangement may be practicable elsewhere. Whether on the inside or the outside wall it is desirable that the toilets should not screen the head of the patient in bed from observation from the corridor, for his feet do not

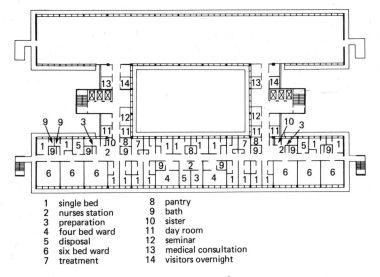

1	single bed	8	pantry
2	nurses station	9	bath
3	preparation	10	sister
4	four bed ward	11	day room
5	disposal	12	seminar
6	six bed ward	13	medical consultation
7	treatment	14	visitors overnight

Wards at Salmaniya hospital, Bahrain. Two wards of sixty beds, each arranged in three units with three nurses' stations, pantries, preparation and disposal rooms. Architects: Llewelyn-Davies Weeks

1	private bed
2	nurses station
3	sister
4	doctor
5	laboratory
6	pantry
7	clean utility
8	treatment
9	day space
10	private patients toilet
11	toilet
12	bath and showers
13	dirty utility/sluice
14	hospital street

Men's wards, each of thirty-two beds, at Maiduguri Teaching Hospital, Nigeria. Two private rooms and the clean nursing ancillary rooms are in the link from the hospital street, but toilets and sluice rooms are in a separate block accessible from both wards and are duplicated. A hot dry climate, the wards face north and south and are naturally ventilated, with screens set back from the external face of the building.

give much indication of his behaviour. In both private and public accommodation this is particularly important for patients who are occupying single rooms because of their medical condition.

For most people it is improbable that the supposed ideal of personal privacy can be economically attainable within the life span of any hospital built today. It is therefore relevant to suggest that, for universal application, privacy is not only an illusory goal for the near future but may also be a very questionable one. This applies both to countries which are trying for the first time to provide facilities for the mass of the population (for whom privacy may well not be something which the life style of the majority of patients leads them to cherish) but also in the more highly developed world where aspirations and expectations tend to encourage it. Contact and involvement may be more valuable than personal isolation.

This hypothesis is unlikely to be proved, but it is at least supported by a recent survey conducted in a London hospital. Comparisons were made between the reactions to three occupied wards that had been built over the past hundred years. In the search for quietness and a less regimented atmosphere, ward design has moved away from the communal Nightingale ward and has established a closer relationship between beds and ancillary rooms. The gains resulting from this may appear self-evident, but it is possible that they have been accompanied by losses.

At St. Thomas' hospital in London, some 19th century Nightingale wards, multi-storey Nuffield type wards of 1966, and air-conditioned multi-bay peripheral wards of 1976 with internal ancillary rooms were all in use simultaneously. During 1976/77 over a period of eighteen months these were the subject of a survey of the opinions of patients, doctors, nursing and other staff to assess the relative degrees of satisfaction offered by the different types.

The results were not as conclusive as might be expected. Although all three types of ward were found to be operating in ways that the users found largely satisfactory it could almost be inferred that the level of satisfaction was in inverse proportion to the date the accommodation had been built. It was not surprising that doctors and nurses preferred the large and open Nightingale wards for their ease of supervision, observation and control. They used the nurses' time more efficiently and gave greater job satisfaction to the sisters than did the other wards. It was not expected that the patients would have much to say in their favour. The conclusions of the survey team's report included the following words:

'In view of the rejection of the 'Nightingale' type ward in hospital planning since the Nuffield Report of 1955 and the well articulated views that patients hate them it was, however, quite unexpected to find how satisfied patients were with (them). The criticisms that are commonly levelled against such wards were not found to be true here. Patients did not feel a great lack of privacy or lack of dignity, nor were they greatly disturbed by each other. The number who were sometimes disturbed was comparable to those in other wards. Far from finding criticisms, many positive advantages . . . . . emerged. The physical unity and the ease of visual communications meant that everyone, staff and patients, identify very strongly with the ward and with each other. Problems tended to be shared. The sympathy and understanding of the patients for each other and for the nurses was high. Social contacts are easy, both to initiate and to withdraw from. There is plenty going on to watch without the need to actively participate. The resulting high community morale is enjoyable and beneficial for the patients.'

These conclusions do not necessarily suggest a return to the original form of the Nightingale ward. They underline the belief that there are other considerations besides privacy and that to some degree its absence may be helpful to patients. It would be hazardous to assume that patients anywhere in the world or drawn from different social groupings would respond in the same way. However, it is hard to dismiss the possibility that, for a high proportion of average short-stay patients, there are indications that the supposed ideal of a private room and a private toilet is not only economically unrealistic but is also therapeutically questionable and would do little or nothing to help their rapid recovery. Besides aiming for compactness and convenience, future developments in ward planning may well concentrate on imparting a sense of community.

0   9 m
0   30 ft

1	single bed	10	sluice
2	nurses station	11	clean utility
3	day room	12	pantry
4	four bed ward	13	clinical investigation
5	bath	14	seminar
6	six bed ward	15	student laboratory
7	sister	16	supply
8	treatment	17	disposal
9	dirty utility		

1   single bed
2   nurses station
3   treatment
4   four bed ward
5   sluice
6   disposal
7   bath
8   toilet
9   day room
10 sister
11 doctors/students
12 visitors
13 pantry
14 utility

0   9 m
           30 ft

A twenty-eight bed Nuffield type ward at St Thomas' Hospital (1966) with one central nurses' station. Architect: W. F. Howitt

A twenty-eight bed ward with one nurses' station at St Thomas' Hospital (1976), comprising one quarter of the floor of a rectangular air-conditioned building. Architects: York Rosenberg Mardall

Chapter 5
Principal departments of the hospital

Categories of accommodation

A hospital comprises three categories of accommodation:

medical services which provide diagnosis and treatment for inpatients and outpatients;

medical support services essential for sustaining the medical services and closely related to them functionally;

general support services which are responsible for general administration, the supply of food, linen and stores, the disposal of waste and the maintenance of heating, lighting and energy, piped supplies and mechanical aids.

Each of these three categories is made up of a number of distinct departments. Every hospital will include some departments from each category but few hospitals will include all departments.

In the *medical services* group the principal departments in addition to the various in-patient wards are:

outpatient clinics,
accident and emergency,
short stay wards associated with accident and emergency,
day units for psychiatric or geriatric patients.

The specialist diagnostic and treatment services, most of which deal with both inpatients and outpatients, are:

diagnostic radiology,
physical medicine,
dentistry,
radiotherapy,
renal dialysis,
the operating department,
the pathology laboratories.

Medical support services comprise:

the pharmacy,
central sterile supply,
a central milk kitchen associated with maternity wards,
the medical library,
central medical records.

General support services are:

central administration,
general supply and disposal,
linen supply and disposal (which may include a laundry),
the mortuary,
catering,
engineering services including maintenance,
transport,
staff changing rooms and amenities (which may include residential accommodation).

A detailed description of all departments is beyond the scope of this book. There is an extensive literature on the subject and the bibliography on page 118 includes some of the more useful publications of a general nature. This chapter is confined to an outline of the function of some of the principal departments and of the basic procedures likely to be followed within them. A brief description is included of the type of accommodation which the needs of each department demand and of their relationship to other departments and their desirable location within the hospital. Although descriptions are based on the British practice at the scale of the district general or regional hospital, many of the techniques are recognised internationally. The functions and procedures are relevant both in the UK and abroad.

The plans that illustrate the departments are not meant to be interpreted as models or in any sense as standards. The requirements of different hospitals will vary as to size and the particulars of accommodation and operational policies. The intention is only to show some relatively recent solutions; read in conjunction with the text they may help readers to visualise the procedures and the functional arrangements to which they give rise.

Out-Patients

The function of the department is to diagnose and to treat home-based patients and if necessary to accept them as in-patients. A good deal of the diagnostic and treatment accommodation can be of a general nature used at different clinic sessions by different specialists. Too much separate accommodation for specialisms is wasteful, for much of it will be underused most of the time.

Organisation is greatly facilitated and overcrowding reduced if out-patients are filtered by a general practitioner, clinic or health centre and proceed (by appointment) to the department only when it is essential. This method is generally known as a referral system. In some countries it may be advisable to have a separate general practitioners clinic adjoining the hospital specifically for this purpose in order to prevent the department (and indeed other parts of the hospital) from becoming grossly overloaded.

For some patients the department will be their first introduction to hospital and many may be nervous and need reassurance. It is important that the atmosphere should be welcoming, comfortable and humane. In a large department, or if there is no adequate referral or appointment system to control the influx of patients, there will be special design problems in retaining a human scale in the arrangement of the large reception and waiting spaces that are likely to be necessary. In some climates shaded open-air areas may be valuable.

The department should be situated so that it is easily reached by both the walking public and vehicles. It should also be close to public transport routes if there are any. A separate entrance is desirable and this should not be located too near the reception point for ambulance and accidents or other departments, such as the mortuary, which are likely to have disturbing associations. Out-patients should not have to pass through any other part of the hospital to reach the department.

It is an advantage if the out-patients department can be entirely at street level, for some patients may find movement difficult. Expansion may need to be anticipated, particularly in developing countries where the facility is being provided for the first time. In countries where local health centres or community hospitals are well established or are increasing steadily in number the future need may be not so much for growth as for change, as the out-patient clinics become more specialised.

Procedure is similar to that in a health centre except that diagnostic techniques and treatment will be more sophisticated. The sequence is

reception,
registration,
waiting,
consultation.

In some cases treatment, or referral to another specialist department may be necessary. Prescriptions may be collected at a dispensary on the way out. It is essential to have an enquiry or registration point at the entrance, associated with a general waiting space.

Many of the people waiting may be relatives or friends who may not wish to accompany patients to the actual clinic. Sub-waiting spaces adjoining the clinic to which patients are directed are desirable and the checking of records may be done there. These reduce the scale of the general waiting space and assist the flow of patients through the department. Patients' toilets and telephones should be associated with all waiting areas, with perhaps a refreshment counter, a shop and a childrens' playroom at the general waiting space.

Usually most of the consulting suites are general purpose, consisting either of ranges of combined consulting and examination rooms or of smaller consulting rooms with examination rooms adjoining. Some specialities may need rooms designed for a particular purpose. A clinical room is required for treatments such as dressings, a room for urine tests etc, clean and dirty utility rooms and sister's office. An operating suite for minor surgical conditions may be needed, together with day space and a day ward in which patients can recover before going home. Although proximity is desirable, this suite need not be immediately adjoining the department.

Normally there is no need to segregate the sexes in an out-patient department but in some countries segregation may be required. This will inevitably lead to an increase in area and to complications in planning the circulation routes and waiting spaces.

The department needs easy access to the radio-diagnostic facilities, to the dispensary, and if possible to physiotherapy. Out-patients may have to visit any or all of these. Although these departments also serve the rest of the hospital it is an advantage if access to them can be as little associated as possible with other main routes within the hospital. Out-patients can easily get lost and stray into areas from which they should be excluded. Proximity to the pathology laboratories is also desirable for the delivery of specimens.

In some developing countries a major out-patient facility in a new hospital can be much sought after by those who are within reach of it. There may well be a problem in controlling the large crowds who will descend on it and in preventing them from penetrating

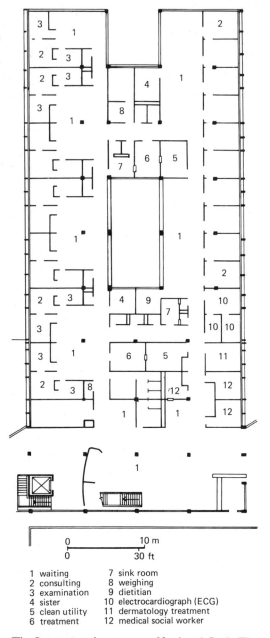

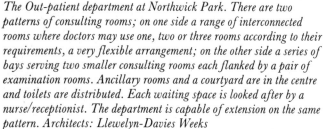

1 waiting	7 sink room
2 consulting	8 weighing
3 examination	9 dietitian
4 sister	10 electrocardiograph (ECG)
5 clean utility	11 dermatology treatment
6 treatment	12 medical social worker

The Out-patient department at Northwick Park. There are two patterns of consulting rooms; on one side a range of interconnected rooms where doctors may use one, two or three rooms according to their requirements, a very flexible arrangement; on the other side a series of bays serving two smaller consulting rooms each flanked by a pair of examination rooms. Ancillary rooms and a courtyard are in the centre and toilets are distributed. Each waiting space is looked after by a nurse/receptionist. The department is capable of extension on the same pattern. Architects: Llewelyn-Davies Weeks

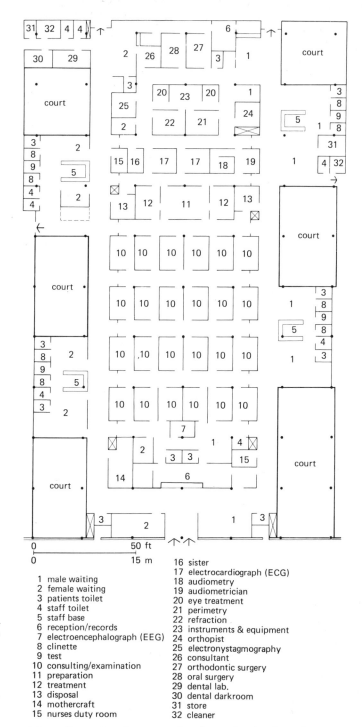

1 male waiting	16 sister
2 female waiting	17 electrocardiograph (ECG)
3 patients toilet	18 audiometry
4 staff toilet	19 audiometrician
5 staff base	20 eye treatment
6 reception/records	21 perimetry
7 electroencephalograph (EEG)	22 refraction
8 clinette	23 instruments & equipment
9 test	24 orthopist
10 consulting/examination	25 electronystagmography
11 preparation	26 consultant
12 treatment	27 orthodontic surgery
13 disposal	28 oral surgery
14 mothercraft	29 dental lab.
15 nurses duty room	30 dental darkroom
	31 store
	32 cleaner

A large Out-patient department for a hospital in Saudi Arabia. Segregation of the sexes is necessary but a degree of flexibility in the allocation of consulting rooms to male or female clinics is desirable. Male and female waiting spaces can be kept entirely separate, and by closing doors at the end of the access corridors the consulting rooms can be used for either sex in any proportion. Architects: Architects' Co-Partnership

into other parts of the building. If there is no adjacent GP clinic to act as a filter a more distinct separation of out-patients from the rest of the hospital may be an advantage, in spite of the close relationships which are desirable with other departments. Ample waiting space will be needed outside the department to accommodate the multitude, many of whom may gather there as much for the social occasion as for medical reasons. This space can be in the open, but should be covered. It is likely that there will be a need for a secure method of containing the waiting crowd and of admitting them to the department in small batches.

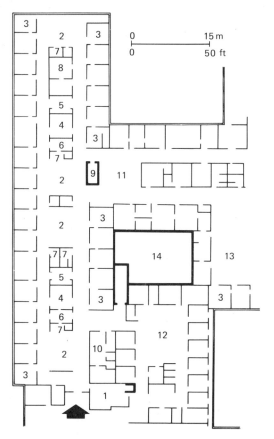

1 reception
2 sub-waiting and clinic receptionist
3 consulting/examination
4 treatment
5 clean supply
6 dirty utility
7 toilets
8 electrocardiograph (ECG)
9 audiometry
10 pathology outstation
11 sub-waiting, ophthalmology and dentistry
12 ante-natal clinic waiting
13 outpatient general surgery waiting
14 services shaft

At Greenwich District Hospital the Outpatient department is approached from the hospital's main entrance and waiting area, where there is a shop, a cafeteria, a children's playroom and a dispensary. It shares the pathology out-station with the adjoining ante-natal clinic. The main part of the department consists of ranges of intercommunicating consulting/examination rooms on both sides of a central core of ancillary rooms and sub-waiting areas. Each of the waiting areas is looked after by a clinic receptionist. An arm containing accommodation for ophthalmology and dentistry, with its own sub-waiting area, leads to a further waiting area that serves a group of rooms and a day ward for minor surgery. Architect: W. E. Tatton Brown, Department of Health and Social Security, with the S. E. Metropolitan Regional Health Board

Accident and emergency

Injury or sudden illness beyond the capacity of the first-aid box drives most people to a doctor or, if they are near a hospital, to its Accident and Emergency department, where they expect immediate attention and reassurance. All hospitals must be able to deal with casualties and emergencies without mixing them with other out-patients. For this they need as a minimum a waiting space, a consulting room, examination and treatment cubicles, a small operating theatre and a few beds for recovery.

Many hospitals will, however, be designated as major accident centres and the department will be much more heavily loaded and will require additional and more sophisticated facilities. Some of the accommodation may differ with the locality, for the type of risks to which the population is exposed will not necessarily be the same in all places and the incidence of cases such as burns, fractures and road accidents may vary. Other units in the vicinity may provide particular specialities, notably in a large urban area.

Because the department deals with patients who are the victims of accidents or sudden illness it is subjected to unpredictable peaks of activity at any time of the day or night. Incoming patients may be ambulant or brought by vehicle. They may come direct or may be referred by a doctor. After examination (which may include X-ray) or resuscitation, patients may be treated within the department and either kept under observation and discharged after a few hours or may be transferred to the wards. Others may go direct to the wards after diagnosis. After discharge some patients may return to the department for follow-up examination or treatment. Certain injuries may have to be referred to specialist hospitals elsewhere.

Because seriously injured patients should be kept separate from others the department requires two independent entrances from outside, one for walking patients and the other for those brought by ambulance. If the unit includes an orthopaedic clinic a third entrance may be desirable, via the out-patients department if the orthopaedic records are kept there.

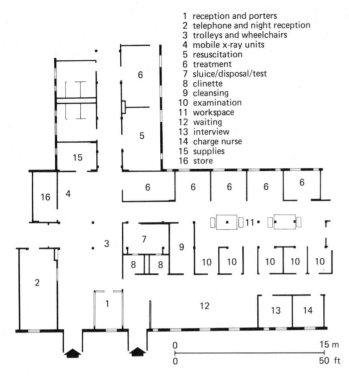

1 reception and porters
2 telephone and night reception
3 trolleys and wheelchairs
4 mobile x-ray units
5 resuscitation
6 treatment
7 sluice/disposal/test
8 clinette
9 cleansing
10 examination
11 workspace
12 waiting
13 interview
14 charge nurse
15 supplies
16 store

The Accident and Emergency department for a Mark 2 'Best Buy' hospital. There are separate entrances for stretcher and walking patients controlled by the same reception and porters room. The ambulance entrance leads to a generous marshalling space and the walking entrance to a waiting area from which small examination cubicles are directly accessible. On the other side of the central workspace and approached from the ambulance entrance there are larger treatment cubicles for patients on trolleys. Architects: McDonald, Hamilton and Montefiore, with the Department of Health and Social Security

Walking patients are either attending for the first time or are coming for follow-up procedures. After reception at a counter where particulars are taken or checked, patients in these two categories can, in a large department, be separated into two distinct waiting areas, sharing lavatories, telephones and perhaps a tea bar. A separate waiting room for children may be desirable.

The ambulance entrance, distinct from the walking patients' entrance, should preferably be enclosed and heated and should lead into a stretcher lobby attended by porters. A room for cases needing emergency treatment or resuscitation should open directly from this lobby. Provision should be made for people accompanying a casualty who, although not themselves injured, may be in a distressed condition.

The main examination, diagnosis and treatment area should be directly accessible from the general waiting areas and the stretcher lobby. The area comprises a number of cubicles, partitioned or curtained or a mixture of both, some large enough for

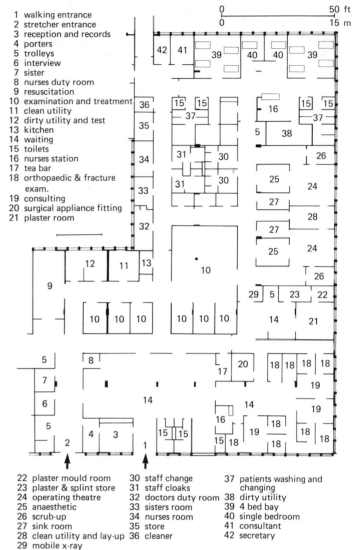

1 walking entrance
2 stretcher entrance
3 reception and records
4 porters
5 trolleys
6 interview
7 sister
8 nurses duty room
9 resuscitation
10 examination and treatment
11 clean utility
12 dirty utility and test
13 kitchen
14 waiting
15 toilets
16 nurses station
17 tea bar
18 orthopaedic & fracture exam.
19 consulting
20 surgical appliance fitting
21 plaster room

22 plaster mould room	30 staff change	37 patients washing and changing
23 plaster & splint store	31 staff cloaks	38 dirty utility
24 operating theatre	32 doctors duty room	39 4 bed bay
25 anaesthetic	33 sisters room	40 single bedroom
26 scrub-up	34 nurses room	41 consultant
27 sink room	35 store	42 secretary
28 clean utility and lay-up	36 cleaner	
29 mobile x-ray		

A major Accident and Emergency department at the King Edward Memorial Hospital, Ealing. The entrance for walking patients leads to a large waiting area with an alcove for children, from which the orthopaedic and fracture section, with its own sub-waiting area, is directly accessible. The reception and records counter communicates with the porters station for stretcher cases from the ambulance entrance. Opposite the porters there is a trolley park, and straight ahead a large resuscitation room and a sub-waiting space for patients on trolleys. Much of the main examination and treatment workspace is flexibly subdivided. The department includes a pair of operating theatres and a ward of ten beds for preparation, recovery or short stay observation. Architect: John R. Harris

patients' trolleys or stretchers, with sluice and utility facilities serving them. The department's own X-ray diagnostic unit with dark room and X-ray viewing area should be adjacent unless the hospital's main X-ray diagnostic department is closely accessible.

If the department has its own operating suite it should be adjacent, probably containing two theatres with scrub-up and gowning rooms, an anaesthetic room and disposal room. A plaster room for the reduction of fractures and the application and removal of plaster casts should be near the operating suite. If all the hospital's operating theatres are centralised there must be quick access to them. In any case it is essential to have quick access to the Intensive Therapy Unit. If the department includes an orthopaedic and fracture clinic, consulting rooms and additional examination and treatment cubicles will be necessary. These should preferably be located near the plaster room, and approached through a waiting space adjoining but distinct from the main follow-up patients' waiting area.

After treatment or operation, and before discharge or admission as an in-patient, some patients will be taken to a small recovery ward in the department. This is a short-stay unit equipped with the usual ward ancillaries on a reduced scale. Patients are unlikely to stay here longer than twenty-four hours.

The department constitutes a highly concentrated unit in which internal relationships are of particular importance in emergencies and lucid planning is vital. This concentration must be combined with generous circulation space to allow easy movement of patients on trolleys or stretchers, as severely injured patients must not be disturbed more than is necessary.

A situation at road level is essential for the reception of emergencies and walking patients, and proximity to the out-patients' department may be an advantage. There must be easy, but not necessarily close, access to the wards for patients on trolleys. If the unit is remote from the hospital's X-ray diagnostic department, as it may have to be, it will require its own X-ray facilities. It will also need a small pathology laboratory if it is remote from the Pathology Department.

Radiodiagnostic

The department receives in-patients, out-patients and casualties. Its function is to photograph, process the film and provide facilities for its interpretation and storage. Patients may arrive on foot, in wheelchairs or on trolleys, and may be wearing dressing gowns, theatre gowns or their normal clothes. After registration they may need to wait, to change their clothes or to undergo preparatory procedures before their X-ray, and following the X-ray they may need a short period for recovery.

X-ray rooms are equipped with photographic machinery of considerable sophistication (some of which is large and heavy and incorporates moving parts needing floor tracks and ceiling support). The

recent introduction of computer linked scanners, which replace the use of X-rays, has introduced a new element into the design of these departments, although in general it has made little change in the total area needed for them. The X-ray rooms need

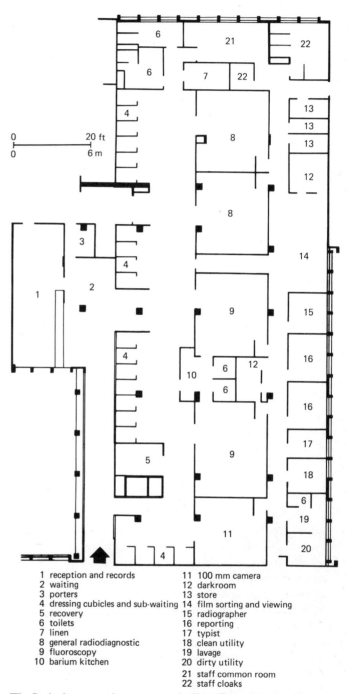

1 reception and records	11 100 mm camera
2 waiting	12 darkroom
3 porters	13 store
4 dressing cubicles and sub-waiting	14 film sorting and viewing
5 recovery	15 radiographer
6 toilets	16 reporting
7 linen	17 typist
8 general radiodiagnostic	18 clean utility
9 fluoroscopy	19 lavage
10 barium kitchen	20 dirty utility
	21 staff common room
	22 staff cloaks

The Radiodiagnostic department at the King Edward Memorial Hospital, Ealing, located adjacent to Accident and Emergency and close to Outpatients. The X-ray rooms form the core, flanked on one side by a reception and records office which commands the entrance to the patients' sub-waiting areas and dressing cubicles, and on the other by processing, viewing and staff rooms. Architect: John R. Harris

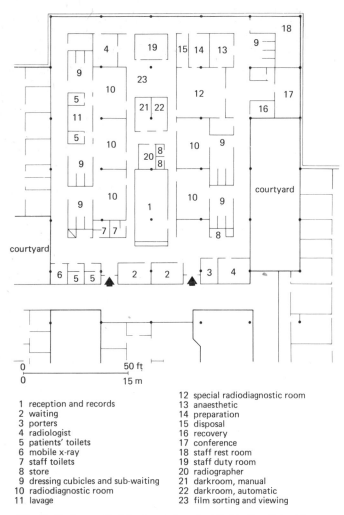

1 reception and records
2 waiting
3 porters
4 radiologist
5 patients' toilets
6 mobile x-ray
7 staff toilets
8 store
9 dressing cubicles and sub-waiting
10 radiodiagnostic room
11 lavage
12 special radiodiagnostic room
13 anaesthetic
14 preparation
15 disposal
16 recovery
17 conference
18 staff rest room
19 staff duty room
20 radiographer
21 darkroom, manual
22 darkroom, automatic
23 film sorting and viewing

The Radiodiagnostic department for a hospital in Saudi Arabia, located between Accident and Emergency and the Operating department and close to the specialist clinics. There are separate sub-waiting and changing areas for each radiodiagnostic room. Architects: Architects' Co-Partnership

Adequate waiting space of a cheerful and unclinical character adjoining the reception office is needed for ambulant and wheelchair patients. There must also be space for in-patients on trolleys. Toilets should adjoin the waiting space. A nurse will normally escort patients to the appropriate X-ray or preparation room. Some serial examinations may be spread over several hours with intervals of waiting between them, and for these separate sitting rooms for each sex are desirable. The traffic of patients' trolleys, equipment and people within the department is likely to be considerable.

Special precautions are necessary with X-ray machines to minimise the risks of irradiation to which staff are exposed. The controls to the X-ray tube are operated from behind a protective screen. The tube is normally capable of pointing vertically downwards or horizontally. The layout of the room depends partly on the equipment, but the basic principle is that the tube should never be able to be pointed towards the control unit or a door, or towards the dark room if it is adjacent.

The location of the department should be convenient for trolley access from the wards and close to the out-patients' department. Unless the Accident and Emergency department has its own X-ray facilities, it is essential that there should be easy access to the X-ray department. It is of advantage to other patients if the reception of accidents can be kept separate from the general waiting spaces. The department is not associated with radiotherapy, which is an entirely different technique. Expansion and change should be anticipated.

Physical medicine

The function of the department is the rehabilitation of patients. It comprises two related sections;
    physiotherapy
    occupational therapy.
Physiotherapy is principally treatment by massage, exercise, heat or electricity for the restoration, for instance, of the function of limbs, sometimes after injury or surgery, or for the education towards independence of patients with severe physical disabilities.

Occupational therapy is the treatment of physical and mental disorders by means of craft or manufacturing activities, frequently related to the patients' lifestyle outside hospital.

The functions of the two sections overlap: both deal with in-patients and out-patients but the latter predominate.

dark rooms nearby for the processing of the films (which may be taken there either manually or by conveyor) and a room for viewing and film sorting.

Ancillary accommodation includes rooms for meetings and conferences, reception and records with arrangements for the storage of current exposed films, offices for radiologists, radiographers and secretaries, general storage and utility rooms, staff cloakrooms, and ample changing cubicles near the X-ray rooms for patients who arrive fully dressed. Some radiodiagnostic procedures are carried out under a general anaesthetic and appropriate facilities and accommodation need to be provided. Barium examinations require separate preparation rooms for rectal washouts, with toilets immediately adjoining, and small recovery rooms in which out-patients can rest before leaving the hospital.

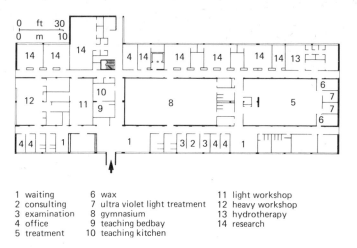

1 waiting
2 consulting
3 examination
4 office
5 treatment
6 wax
7 ultra violet light treatment
8 gymnasium
9 teaching bedbay
10 teaching kitchen
11 light workshop
12 heavy workshop
13 hydrotherapy
14 research

The Physical Medicine department at Northwick Park Hospital and Clinical Research Centre. There is an independent main entrance for outpatients but it is also entered direct from the hospital. The central core of the department contains heavy and light workshops, teaching kitchen, bed bay and bathroom, gymnasium, and a large treatment area off which open smaller rooms for wax and ultra violet light treatment. The department includes a range of research laboratories. Architects: Llewelyn-Davies Weeks

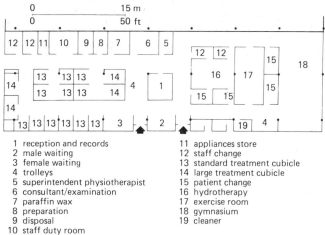

1 reception and records
2 male waiting
3 female waiting
4 trolleys
5 superintendent physiotherapist
6 consultant/examination
7 paraffin wax
8 preparation
9 disposal
10 staff duty room
11 appliances store
12 staff change
13 standard treatment cubicle
14 large treatment cubicle
15 patient change
16 hydrotherapy
17 exercise room
18 gymnasium
19 cleaner

The Physical Medicine department for a hospital in Saudi Arabia. The treatment area is sub-divided into bays to provide the opportunity of dealing with male and female patients with some degree of privacy. In addition to the gynmasium there is a separate exercise room, primarily for children who have suffered cerebral palsy. The department is close to the specialist clinics and is entered only from within the hospital. Occupational therapy is located elsewhere with a psychiatric day unit. Architects: Architects' Co-Partnership

Physical medicine should be close to the out-patients' department, from which it should, if possible, be directly accessible. In-patients also need to be able to reach it easily without passing through the out-patients' waiting areas. As many patients will arrive by vehicle road access is necessary. Throughout the department the planning must take particular account of the requirements of wheelchair users and of others with disabilities that make movement difficult.

The physiotherapy accommodation consists of two distinct areas; one for passive treatment such as massage or radiant heat, and the other for treatment requiring the patient's active participation, such as exercise in a gymnasium or movement in a hydrotherapy pool. From the reception and waiting space patients pass either to male or female changing rooms and thence to the passive treatment section or to the gymnasium. Alternatively, they may go direct to the pool, which will have its own changing rooms.

The passive treatment section consists of a number of separate rooms or cubicles or, alternatively and more flexibly, one area subdivided by adjustable curtains. Its ancillary spaces are a small bay for the preparation of dressings, etc and a room for paraffin wax treatment and plaster splint making.

In the active treatment section the gymnasium is conventional, preferably high enough for ball games and if possible with access to a terrace for exercise in the open air. The hydrotherapy pool is raised like a bath above the pool surround so that staff can handle

patients; it is entered by a flight of steps. In addition to changing cubicles, lockers, toilets and showers it needs staff changing space, a utility room for rinsing, drying and dry storage, and a rest room where patients can lie down after treatment.

Three distinct areas are customary for occupational therapy:

a heavy workshop for woodwork and light metalwork supervised by a technician, which is likely to be relatively noisy;

a light workshop for handicrafts and clerical rehabilitation including typewriting;

a domestic section for re-education, particularly of the disabled, in the everyday activities of getting in and out of bed, bathing and using a toilet and working in the kitchen.

In all these areas some patients are likely to be working in wheelchairs. The workshops need storage space for raw materials and equipment, and for finished products. In some hospitals there may also be a need for gardening facilities immediately adjoining the department.

Maternity

Faced with sudden injury, incapacity or pain, most people in most countries will turn to a hospital for help if they can . But faced with childbirth the reaction may be different, for custom, religion, superstition and

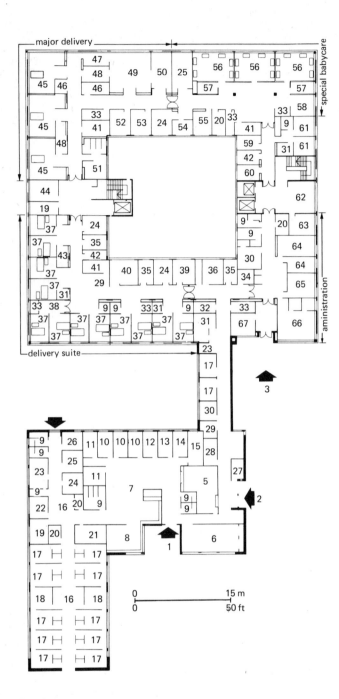

1 clinic entrance and pram park
2 admissions entrance
3 visitors entrance
4 service entrance
5 records
6 mothercraft
7 waiting and tea bar
8 children's waiting
9 toilet
10 history taking
11 blood taking
12 medical social worker
13 health visitor
14 district midwife
15 medical staff
16 sub-waiting
17 examination
18 consulting
19 sister
20 cleaner
21 linen and equipment
22 consultant paedetrician
23 clinette
24 clean utility
25 treatment
26 dirty utility
27 porter
28 flying squad
29 nurses station
30 visitors
31 bath
32 utility
33 linen
34 GPs coats
35 sluice
36 GP admissions
37 first stage/delivery
38 soundproof lobby
39 sink room test
40 dayroom
41 equipment
42 pantry
43 toilet and shower
44 duty room
45 delivery
46 sterile room
47 scrub-up
48 sink room
49 theatre
50 anaesthetic
51 female changing
52 male changing
53 doctors duty room
54 milk pantry
55 demonstration
56 six cots
57 single cot
58 doctor/sister
59 gowning/scrub-up
60 dirty utility
61 mother's bedroom
62 visitors waiting
63 nurses cloaks
64 midwifery suptd.
65 consultant
66 clerical office
67 admin. staff room

Ground floor of the Maternity department at Chase Farm Hospital, Enfield. The ante-natal clinic is a single storey building and is linked to a three storey in-patient block. There are separate entrances for clinic, admissions and for visitors, each leading to clearly defined territories.

In the clinic the history and blood taking rooms open off the main waiting area. The examination rooms are ranged along a separate corridor and are entered by patients through undressing cubicles and *by doctors through intercommunicating doors. The records office serves both the clinic waiting area and the inpatient admissions entrance.*

The inpatient floor comprises four territories: a group of twelve first stage and delivery rooms grouped around a nurses' station, three larger rooms and a theatre for major deliveries, a special care baby unit, and an administrative unit through which visitors enter to reach the lying-in wards on the two upper floors. Architects: Stillman and Eastwick-Field

family pressures intervene. The need for and the attitude towards institutionalised help varies widely from one country to another, but where maternity facilities are provided (and they must be provided for some pregnancies) certain basic requirements are universal.

Unlike most other departments of the hospital the maternity department is normally concerned with a natural rather than a pathological event. It is also dealing with a continuous process, from pregnancy through delivery to after-care of both mother and child. It is not principally concerned with curing a condition but with fulfilling it. Thus not only are its accommodation requirements different from those of other wards but it is important that it should not be associated psychologically with illness.

For this reason, and to avoid risks of infection to newly born babies, it is greatly to be preferred if the maternity department can to some degree be separate from the rest of the hospital, perhaps not geographically but certainly with its own entrance. It should retain close communication links with the hospital for meals and supplies and reasonable links with other departments to which mothers may sometimes need access.

Whatever its size the department has two main parts; the *out-patient clinic* and the accommodation for *in-patient delivery and aftercare*. The clinic, which may be associated with the out-patients' department or may be separate, is primarily ante-natal. Depending on the arrangements of the particular hospital and the attitude of the gynaecologists and obstetricions concerned, the same rooms may serve for post-natal examinations, family planning consultations and gynaecological out-patients.

Ante-natal patients are usually seen at the time of booking, at about the thirty sixth week of pregnancy, and then weekly until admission for delivery. This clinic will preferably be approached separately from the department's ambulance entrance, and the accommodation will comprise a waiting space, rooms for history taking and examination with three or four undressing cubicles to each room, a urine testing room and lavatory, and space for offices and records. Easy access to the X-ray department and to pathology is an advantage.

The ante-natal clinic should have a non-clinical atmosphere, for in many areas it provides a valuable social meeting place for expectant mothers. This function can be of particular importance in new communities.

The in-patient accommodation falls into two closely related divisions, one concerned with labour and birth and the other with the lying-in wards. The labour suite, which should be accessible wihout passing through the wards, consists of first-stage rooms, each with one bed, and delivery rooms, both on a scale of one room to about ten post-natal beds. Pairs of delivery rooms can share wash-up and scrub-up.

If there is no separate operating theatre for the department, or the hospital's main operating suite is not nearby, one delivery room needs to be suitable for caesarian operations, with scrub-up and anaesthetising room adjoining. The delivery rooms should be well insulated acoustically from the first-stage rooms and from the ward. A comfortable day room for visitors is needed near the entrance to the labour suite.

The ward has day room and ancillaries similar to a normal ward except that a treatment room is unlikely to be needed. It will probably be divided into four or six bedded rooms with perhaps about a quarter to a third of the mothers in single rooms. Cots beside the mother's beds, or 'rooming-in', is usually preferred to a central nursery because it presents less risk of cross infection. Some countries adopt an arrangement in which a small nursery is situated between each pair of two or three bedded rooms, with communicating doors.

In addition a Special Care Baby Unit, capable of temperature and in some countries humidity control, should be provided. This consists of separate rooms, each containing about six cots, and incubators, an isolation facility, and a gowning room for staff entering the unit.

A central milk kitchen is required, divided into a clean room for the preparation of milk feeds and the sterilisation of equipment, and a dirty room for wash-up. In a very large department it may be convenient to provide more than one kitchen, for instance on each ward floor. Cleanliness is of critical importance here, for newly born babies have little immunity from infection.

Operating theatres

The function of the department is to receive patients after diagnosis, to anaesthetise them either before or after transfer to the operating table, to operate, and to supervise their post-operative condition before returning them to the wards.

The department consists of one or more operating suites which share ancillary accommodation such as staff changing and rest rooms, arrangements for the reception of patients, and facilities for the disposal of soiled material. The suites may also share a unit for the supply of sterile material and instruments. Each operating suite normally consists of a theatre, an anaesthetic room, a preparation room and a scrub-up.

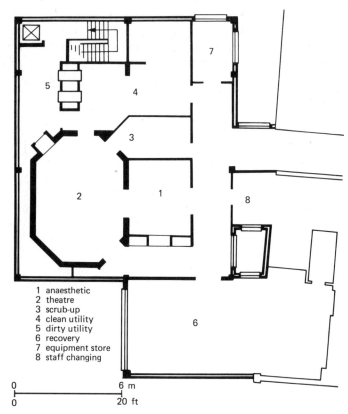

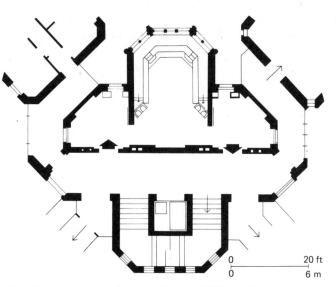

1 anaesthetic
2 theatre
3 scrub-up
4 clean utility
5 dirty utility
6 recovery
7 equipment store
8 staff changing

A single theatre addition at the London Hospital, Mile End. A clean access corridor provides the approach to the suite for patients, staff and stores, and for the patient's transfer to the Recovery Room after the operation. Soiled material from the theatre is passed through a hatch to the dirty utility room for disposal by lift or, after washing, for autoclaving and retrieval in the clean utility room on the other side. The door between dirty and clean utility rooms is for emergency use. Architects: T. P. Bennett & Son

The original operating theatre, built about 1900, at University College Hospital, London. With entrance through an anaesthetic room and exit through a recovery room, from which it can be separated by sliding doors, it is conveniently but somewhat dangerously located off the main circulation core of the building. Steeply tiered seating allows spectators close observation of the procedure and there are basins for the surgeons to wash themselves. Architect: Alfred Waterhouse

In some countries it is the practice to anaesthetise in the theatre itself.

For reasons of staffing, engineering services, flexibility of programming and the sharing of ancillaries operating suites are usually located together in one department if possible. Operations for accidents and emergencies, and sometimes for maternity, may need to be located elsewhere, and there may be an independent suite for minor operations, principally associated with the out-patients' department. Accident and emergency cases needing major surgery will nevertheless probably be dealt with in the main operating department.

Before the introduction of shadowless artificial lighting, surgery used to need adequate natural light and for this reason many operating departments have customarily been located on a top floor. Today good light and good ventilation can be provided artificially and this location is no longer necessary. Indeed the

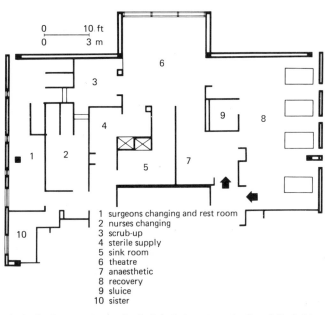

1 surgeons changing and rest room
2 nurses changing
3 scrub-up
4 sterile supply
5 sink room
6 theatre
7 anaesthetic
8 recovery
9 sluice
10 sister

A single theatre suite in the Ophthalmic unit at the Royal Berkshire Hospital, Reading, served by a central sterilising department elsewhere in the building. Staff enter the theatre from their changing rooms via the scrub-up. Supplies reach the sterile supply room by lift from the CSSD and thus direct into the theatre. Soiled material from the theatre is passed into the sink room and is disposed of or taken by separate lift for central sterilization. Patients leave the theatre directly into the recovery ward, which communicates with the clean lobby by which they entered. Architects: Architects' Co-Partnership

vibration that can arise from the proximity of air-conditioning machinery on an upper floor may make it undesirable. In countries where there are dust storms, a top floor location will not necessarily avoid their effect, as dust can be blown up to heights of 50 m or more.

Although the requirements of theatres can be met by an entirely internal situation, from the point of view of staff who spend long periods in the department, some natural light can be a valuable asset. This should be provided for some of the ancillary staff-rooms and should have some prospect of the outside. Whatever the location of the operating theatre, it is important that the communication routes from all the wards (not only the surgical ones, for the balance may change) should be direct, easy and if possible short. The department should be on a *cul-de-sac* so that access to it can be strictly controlled. Access from the accident and emergency department should be particularly easy.

If there is an Intensive Therapy Unit it should be nearby, and preferably adjacent. Proximity to the X-ray diagnostic department is not usually of great importance, for if X-rays are needed during operations the work will normally be done with mobile machines.

It used to be normal practice in Britain to sterilise instruments within the suite, a pair of theatres sharing

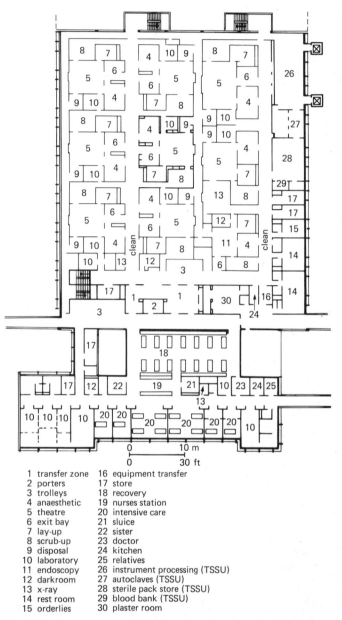

1 transfer zone
2 porters
3 trolleys
4 anaesthetic
5 theatre
6 exit bay
7 lay-up
8 scrub-up
9 disposal
10 laboratory
11 endoscopy
12 darkroom
13 x-ray
14 rest room
15 orderlies
16 equipment transfer
17 store
18 recovery
19 nurses station
20 intensive care
21 sluice
22 sister
23 doctor
24 kitchen
25 relatives
26 instrument processing (TSSU)
27 autoclaves (TSSU)
28 sterile pack store (TSSU)
29 blood bank (TSSU)
30 plaster room

A large operating department at Northwick Park Hospital and Clinical Research Centre, with its own Theatre Sterile Supply Unit and a recovery ward associated with the Intensive Care Unit. There are eight theatres and an endoscopy suite. Patients enter and leave the inner clean zone through a transfer lobby. Entirely separate dirty corridors connect each theatre's disposal room to the TSSU, where instruments are processed, autoclaved and passed into a sterile pack store, from which they are taken via the clean zone to the theatre lay-up rooms. Because of the research function laboratories adjoin the Recovery and Intensive Care Unit and each of the theatres. Architects: Llewelyn-Davies Weeks

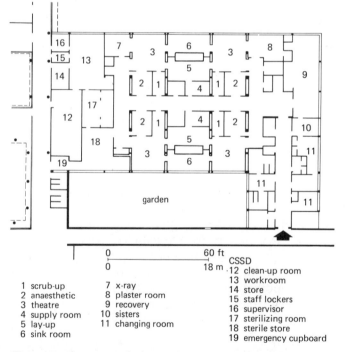

CSSD
1 scrub-up
2 anaesthetic
3 theatre
4 supply room
5 lay-up
6 sink room
7 x-ray
8 plaster room
9 recovery
10 sisters
11 changing room
12 clean-up room
13 workroom
14 store
15 staff lockers
16 supervisor
17 sterilizing room
18 sterile store
19 emergency cupboard

Two pairs of operating theatres with recovery ward at Wexham Park Hospital. Lay-up rooms and sink rooms are separated by autoclaves. The suites adjoin the central sterile supply department, which comprises a clean-up room from which goods are passed into a workroom and thence via the sterilizing room to a sterile store: from this they are distributed either to the hospital or direct to the theatre corridor and the supply rooms that serve each pair of theatres. Architects: Powell and Moya

between them a sink and disposal room which was separated from a sterilizing room by autoclaves. Both sink and sterilizing rooms communicated directly with the theatres. More recently this arrangement has tended to be avoided if possible, not least because of the difficulties it can present for temperature and humidity control in the theatres. Instead cleansing and the supply of sterile goods is done in a separate Theatre Sterile Supply Unit (TSSU) which can serve a larger number of theatres via a small preparation room attached to each of them. Alternatively, if there is a Central Sterile Supply Department (CSSD) for the whole hospital the work can be done there. The method of sterilization and supply affects fundamentally the planning of the department.

Of prime importance in the design of the department is the need to reduce to a minimum the risk of infection at the operating table. This is vital for any operation but has become increasingly important as a result of advances involving deep surgery and lengthy exposure. Ensuring the sterility of instruments and other apparatus is relatively simple, but no less important is the reduction of risks of airborne infection. This depends upon management procedures and the physical arrangement of the department and of its ventilation system. The physical arrangement should ensure that not only are these procedures facilitated but that as far as possible they are inescapable.

The suite can be regarded as a sandwich in which the centre consists of the theatre, the anaesthetic room, the scrub-up in which those working in the theatre can wash and gown, and the supply, preparation or lay-up room through which instruments and materials are passed into the theatre. This centre is flanked on one side by a clean area from which patients, staff and sterile supplies reach the centre, and on the other side by a dirty area or disposal route through which soiled or infected material leaves it. Theatre staff enter the clean area through changing rooms.

To minimise the risk of infection the method of artificial ventilation should ensure that within each suite there is a supply of pure air sufficient to reduce the bacterial count below a critical level. There should be a positive pressure in the theatre and preparation room to provide a flow of air from the clean to the less clean areas. Where there is more than one operating suite in the department, as will usually be the case, each should have its own self-contained ventilation system in order to reduce the risk of cross infection. There should be no movement of air from one suite to another.

Patients are wheeled to the department either in their own beds or on trolleys. They are likely to have received a 'pre-medical' injection in the ward and to be unaware of what is happening. Whether in bed or on trolley they are usually transferred to a theatre trolley in a transfer zone or lobby at the entrance to the department and ample space may be needed outside this zone for a bed or trolley park.

In the UK and some other countries the patient is trolleyed from the transfer zone to the anaesthetic room adjoining the theatre, and after anaesthesia is trolleyed into the theatre and transferred to the operating table. Sometimes the table itself is mobile and the transfer takes place in the anaesthetic room. On the other hand, in the USA and many countries, a separate anaesthetic room is unusual and anaesthesia is induced in the theatre itself. But whether or not there is an anaesthetic room the anaesthetist needs a wide variety of equipment, instruments and drugs which calls for considerable storage space.

After the operation the patient is transferred from the table to a trolley and is wheeled through an exit bay into the clean area and thence to a recovery area. After recovery from the anaesthetic the patient is returned by the route through which he entered, either to his own ward or to the Intensive Therapy Unit if his condition is critical

The recovery area serves all the theatres in the department (assuming that they are all on the same floor). The usual British practice is to provide about three bed spaces for a pair of theatres. Because post-operative conditions may demand constant attention by nurse or anaesthetist, and sometimes visits by the surgeon, the recovery area needs to be easily supervised and readily accessible from the theatres.

The procedures carried out in the operating department are probably the most precise and critical of all the functions performed in a hospital. The suite itself makes the most exacting demands upon detailed design and is frequently the most remote from the average designer's direct experience. Ventilation and lighting are probably open to more refined improvement than in any other part of a hospital building. For these reasons there may be much to be said for a design approach that anticipates future flexibility and change instead of attempting precise original design with materials and equipment that may be difficult to alter later.

There are already available commercially prefabricated operating suite units, analogous to other items of hospital equipment. These integrate the enclosure and its components with the lighting, engineering services and ventilation and can stand like huts or tents within the building structure. It may be that units of this nature are valuable not only for introduction into old buildings where the operating suites no longer provide the facilities necessary for modern surgery, but also for new buildings. In the latter case the prefabricated units can be installed from the outset within an adequately spacious permanent shell in the knowledge that they will function efficiently and in anticipation that even more sophisticated units are likely to supercede them in the future.

Within the theatre itself a further development in the effort to reduce the risk of airborne infection is a glazed sterile enclosure around the operating table. Inside this the operating team can work. The enclosure can be combined with a body exhaust system in which the team wear hoods and gowns connected to an extract system so that they do not contaminate the air within the enclosure.

Intensive therapy

The purpose of the unit, variously known as the Intensive Therapy Unit or Intensive Care Ward, is to give the most highly skilled care to the most acutely ill and to be able to do so continuously and in a concentrated manner throughout the twenty four hours. Its patients are relatively short stay. They may

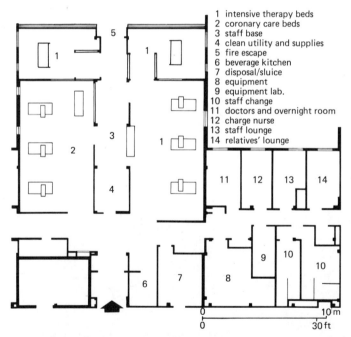

1 intensive therapy beds
2 coronary care beds
3 staff base
4 clean utility and supplies
5 fire escape
6 beverage kitchen
7 disposal/sluice
8 equipment
9 equipment lab.
10 staff change
11 doctors and overnight room
12 charge nurse
13 staff lounge
14 relatives' lounge

The Intensive Therapy Unit in a Mark 2 'Best Buy' hospital. The staff base in the centre of the ward overlooks five intensive therapy beds, of which two are in single rooms with lobby entrances an glazed partitions, and also a separate enclosure for three coronary care beds. Only the clean utility bay communicates directly with the ward; all other ancillary rooms are off the entrance corridor. Architects: McDonald, Hamilton & Montefiore, with the Department of Health and Social Security

be in the unit for perhaps four to eight days before transfer to an ordinary ward if their treatment has been successful. It is entirely different from other wards, for all the patients are bedfast and are likely to be connected to monitoring or life support systems. Their condition demands that they must all be visible all the time and under the constant control of the nursing team.

All necessary services must be readily available at the bedside. Although there is a tendency for some of the equipment to become more compact than it used to be, which makes wall or even ceiling mounting possible and avoids obstructing the bedside, it is still necessary to have generous space around the bed for some bulky specialist machines. Some of the machines are heavy, and wall, floor and ceiling loadings may be critical.

The unit invariably has fewer beds than the normal ward (between 1% and 2% of the total number of acute beds) and will usually not contain more than eighteen beds, broken down into sub-divisions of about six with a small proportion of single rooms for isolation. In addition to clean and dirty utility rooms its ancillary accommodation is likely to include waiting space for relatives, bedroom accommodation for overnight visitors or relatives, additional rooms for staff and generous storage space for portable equipment.

Access to the unit must be strictly controlled. It is usually situated close to the operating theatres and if possible to the Accident and Emergency Department. It has a higher claim to full air-conditioning than do the other wards.

Pathology

The essential function of the department is to carry out diagnostic tests on specimens from in-patients and out-patients. It may also be concerned with work for clinics, health centres, local practitioners and the public health services. Apart from other considerations an efficient laboratory that produces accurate results rapidly can be an important factor in reducing the patients' length of stay and thus contribute substantially to the economy of a hospital.

Within the department the main divisions are those for histology and morbid anatomy, which involve the microscopic examination of tissues and cells; haematology, the study of the blood; bio-chemistry, the study of living tissues and fluids; and micro-biology, the study of micro-organisms. Each of these divisions may require sub-departments, their extent depending on the context and policy of the laboratory.

85

Although each division carries out a different type of work and needs particular ancillary accommodation the boundaries between them tend to become blurred, some techniques may be shared, and the basic laboratory bench requirement does not differ essentially from one to another. A standardised modular plan and a system of service spurs feeding relatively deep bays at right angles to a corridor or open aisle can accept a wide variety of bench arrangements and ancillary spaces and offices. It can also provide reasonable flexibility for the future changes which will undoubtedly be demanded.

In addition to those originating from outside the hospital specimens will be delivered from the wards, the operating theatres, the mortuary, the out-patients'

department, or from the accident and emergency department if it is nearby. Some specimens, particularly blood and urine, will be obtained from out-patients on the spot, and for this a patients' waiting space, lavatories, and several consulting/examination rooms are necessary. Nearly all specimens will pass through a central reception and sorting office before distribution to the appropriate laboratory divisions.

If diagnostic reports are to reach the originator of the request quickly in an emergency, it is clear that the pathology laboratory should ideally be close to the theatres and to accidents. But an overriding consideration may be its relationship to out-patients, not for reasons of speed but for their convenience. However, small ancillary units are often sited in the Intensive

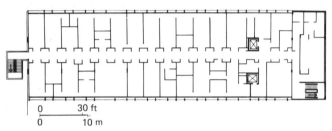

One of the two floors of a large Pathology department at Northwick Park Hospital and Clinical Research Centre. Services run in vertical shafts at a regular module on both sides of the central corridor and feed into the laboratories horizontally on the bench lines, above floor level. Benches and partitions may be rearranged and the functions of individual rooms changed. Internal rooms are cold rooms, centrifuges, dark rooms etc. The external escape stair can be taken down and re-erected if the building is extended. Architects: Llewelyn-Davies Weeks

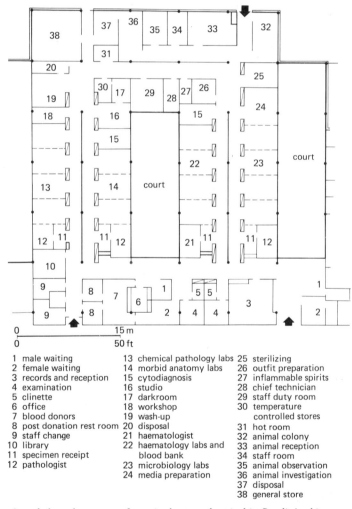

1 male waiting	13 chemical pathology labs	25 sterilizing
2 female waiting	14 morbid anatomy labs	26 outfit preparation
3 records and reception	15 cytodiagnosis	27 inflammable spirits
4 examination	16 studio	28 chief technician
5 clinette	17 darkroom	29 staff duty room
6 office	18 workshop	30 temperature
7 blood donors	19 wash-up	controlled stores
8 post donation rest room	20 disposal	31 hot room
9 staff change	21 haematologist	32 animal colony
10 library	22 haematology labs and	33 animal reception
11 specimen receipt	blood bank	34 staff room
12 pathologist	23 microbiology labs	35 animal observation
	24 media preparation	36 animal investigation
		37 disposal
		38 general store

A pathology department for a single storey hospital in Saudi Arabia. Services are in vertical ducts and run out horizontally along the bench lines as at Northwick Park. Washup and sterilizing are centralised. There is a separate animal house. Outside the laboratory area there is provision for blood donors and the collection of specimens from patients. Architects: Architects' Co-Partnership

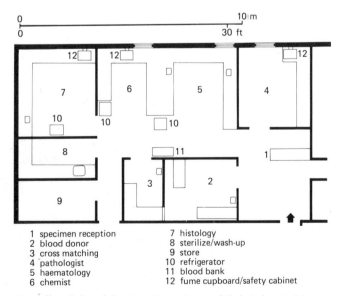

1 specimen reception	7 histology
2 blood donor	8 sterilize/wash-up
3 cross matching	9 store
4 pathologist	10 refrigerator
5 haematology	11 blood bank
6 chemist	12 fume cupboard/safety cabinet

A small pathology laboratory in a private ophthalmic hospital in Saudi Arabia. Architects: Architects' Co-Partnership

Care Ward (for speedy blood gas analysis), in an accident unit, or in out-patient units if they are not close to the main laboratory facilities.

In addition to the likelihood of the department's internal requirements changing it may well need space for expansion. This would be particularly necessary if an increasing role in servicing demands from outside the hospital is to be anticipated.

Pharmaceutical

The pharmacy serves the whole hospital. It stores pharmaceutical products manufactured elsewhere and may also store dressings. It usually manufactures some sterile and non-sterile products in bulk and dispenses prescriptions, sometimes direct to out-patients. It supplies all wards and other departments, often on the basis of daily deliveries. For small

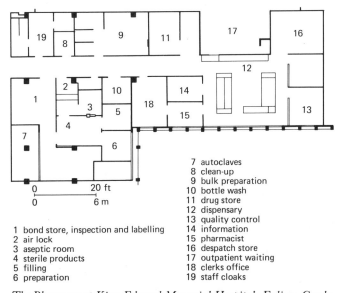

1 bond store, inspection and labelling
2 air lock
3 aseptic room
4 sterile products
5 filling
6 preparation
7 autoclaves
8 clean-up
9 bulk preparation
10 bottle wash
11 drug store
12 dispensary
13 quality control
14 information
15 pharmacist
16 despatch store
17 outpatient waiting
18 clerks office
19 staff cloaks

The Pharmacy at King Edward Memorial Hospital, Ealing. Goods are delivered by road elsewhere in the hospital and reach the pharmacy from within the building. The department is situated next door to Outpatients and has its own sub-waiting space for the collection of prescriptions. Architect: John R. Harris

hospitals, manufacture and dispensing may be done at a larger centre elsewhere and the function of the department may be restricted to storage and distribution.

Because supervision of drugs is essential and security is of first importance, manufactured goods are sometimes received direct by the pharmacy rather than via the hospital's main stores. The basic work flow in the department is reception of goods, unpacking and checking, then storage in either a dressings

store or a drugs store, and finally dispensing and distribution. The reception point needs ample provision for disposable packaging and returnable empties.

Some of the products (poisons and dangerous drugs) require special security measures. Others need refrigeration, and some flammable liquids may demand particular precautions against fire or explosion involving storage outside the building.

From the drugs store, goods pass to the dispensing section either direct or via a bulk preparation room. In the dispensary they are broken down into correct quantities, and from there distributed to the hospital or collected direct at a counter on prescription by out-patients. A separate waiting space is necessary for the latter unless it is combined with the out-patients' main waiting area. Ancillary accommodation includes staff offices and lavatories, a laboratory, and a suite for the manufacture of sterile products comprising preparation room, wash-up, autoclaves, and a room for inspection, labelling and storage.

If the pharmacy is to serve out-patients direct rather than through a separate dispensary proximity to the out-patients department is the main consideration in its location. For this reason it is usually situated at road level. Its relation to the rest of the hospital is relatively unimportant provided it has easy access to the communication routes. Road access for deliveries is highly desirable.

Central sterile supply

A hospital consumes a large quantity of new material that needs sterilisation before use. It also processes other material that has to be cleaned and sterilised before it can be used again. This sterilisation used to be carried out where and when the material was wanted, for instance in the wards or the operating suite. Nowadays items can be supplied by manufacturers in sterilised packs appropriate for particular purposes and an increasing number of them are disposable (which affects both the storage and the disposal areas needed). However, the hospital still needs to sterilise most items and also to control the supply of properly sterilised material to wherever it is needed.

The purpose of a central sterilising department is to concentrate the skill and the responsibility for the supply of this material and to reduce the risk of error. The department also enables the nursing staff to do their work with patients more effectively. Where there are several hospitals in fairly close proximity one department may provide this service for them all.

The department receives clean material from a laundry and new material from manufacturers and suppliers. These deliveries normally arrive by road. It also receives, for re-use, dirty articles from within the hospital. These are normally brought by trolley but may also arrive by road if the department is servicing more than one hospital.

Clean and dirty materials require separate delivery points, the clean one serving a bulk store for new materials such as towels and masks, and the dirty one serving a clean-up room where all re-usable goods including instruments and syringes are washed, cleaned and dried. Rubber gloves may either be dealt with here or passed through the clean-up room to a separate glove room for treatment.

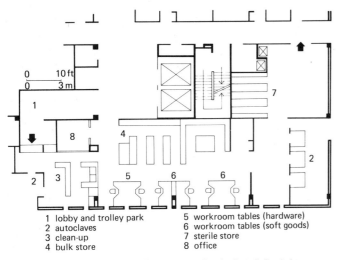

1 lobby and trolley park
2 autoclaves
3 clean-up
4 bulk store
5 workroom tables (hardware)
6 workroom tables (soft goods)
7 sterile store
8 office

The Central Sterile Supply Department for the Royal Berkshire Hospital, Reading. Soiled material from within the hospital arrives on trolleys; from the lobby it is passed across a counter into the clean-up area. Clean material is taken through a doorway direct into the bulk store. Packs are assembled at the tables in the workroom, which is not separated from the storage area; they pass through the autoclave room before reaching the sterile store. The two small lifts adjoining the sterile store serve an ophthalmic operating theatre, one into its preparation room and the other from its disposal room. Architects: Architects' Co-Partnership

From the clean-up room syringes and instruments are passed to another room for inspection, maintenance and dry heat sterilisation before being placed in a sterile store. Other goods pass from the clean-up room, the glove room or the bulk store into a workroom. Here packs are made up and stored temporarily before being autoclaved and taken into a sterile store.

From the sterile store goods are issued to a trolley loading bay for distribution. This will need easy access to a vehicle loading bay if the department is supplying more than one hospital. Except for the delivery and dispatch points the department is planned on a closed circuit production flow. The ancillary rooms for staff communicate with the main workroom.

The department should be in the hospital's service zone to simplify the reception of goods (and of deliveries to other hospitals if it is intended to serve them as well). Proximity to the boiler house is an advantage if steam is raised there. Good communication routes to most of the other departments of the hospital are essential.

The advantages of complete centralisation of sterile supplies do not necessarily extend to the operating department. Here the large number of instruments that are used have customarily been sterilised locally (indeed some of them may be regarded by some surgeons as their personal tools). Nevertheless, it is becoming increasingly recognised that there are advantages in concentrating sterilisation for all the operating suites either in the Central Sterilising Department or in a Theatre Sterile Supply Unit (TSSU) instead of providing separate sterilising facilities for each theatre suite. One of the advantages of this concentration is that the absence of local autoclaves avoids the problem of heat and humidity in the operating suite and simplifies the supply of correctly conditioned air.

Catering

Suitable food well cooked and presented is an important part of the patient's treatment. In the developed world the trend has been towards an increasing degree of individual choice of menu together with dietary supervision. There is an increasing sophistication in the methods of cooking and distribution with the object that meals should reach the patient in as attractive a form as practicable yet demand the minimum amount of labour.

Food has to be supplied to both patients and staff, and in a modern hospital the total number of staff may be roughly equal to the number of beds. One central kitchen usually supplies all the food and because it simplifies service the staff dining rooms are generally sited adjacent to the kitchen.

Several methods are in use for delivery of meals from kitchen to wards. They differ in the method of processing, the palatability, the means of transport and the amount of labour that is necessary. Food may be transported to each ward in a bulk container by heated trolley and served on to plates by the ward staff. This method has for a long time been the normal method and is simple and effective; it allows for immediate adjustments in the quantity given to individual patients but is relatively labour intensive in the wards.

More recent methods are for individual meals to be portioned and plated up in the kitchen or served there on to insulated and compartmented trays, and delivered complete by trolley or conveyor. Alternatively and more rarely food may be cooked centrally, then frozen, and finally reheated in the ward kitchen, or even prepared centrally and cooked in the ward kitchen.

There is an increasing use of bulk frozen foods, with consequent implications on the storage requirements, and also of the bulk purchase of ready-made frozen meals from commercial sources. The catering may be run by the hospital or contracted out to external organisations. The different methods are reflected in the size, equipment and planning of both central and ward kitchens. Only conveyor delivery is likely to affect fundamentally the strategic planning of the building, tending to put a premium on concentration and vertical stacking. This system is fairly widely adopted in the USA but it demands a high degree of technical efficiency and is unlikely to be relevant to any but the most sophisticated and mechanically dependent hospitals.

The washing up of crockery and utensils has in the past been done in the ward kitchens. This is now usually centralised in the main kitchen, with the advantages of more efficient steam sterilisation, less work for the ward staff and less noise in the ward itself.

In some countries it is usual, for economic, cultural or religious reasons, for friends or relatives to supply patients' meals, bringing in food from their homes if they live nearby. It is sometimes customary for members of the family to accompany a patient to hospital and to stay in the vicinity or even in the ward until he is discharged, purchasing, cooking and serving his food. Sometimes simple communal visitors' cookhouses are provided for this purpose outside the hospital.

This practice seems likely to continue, particularly in rural hospitals. Provided there is control over what the patient is permitted to eat there seems little reason to change it, for family support can be of importance to a patient's recovery besides easing the burden on the hospital. Where these practices are general some much reduced provision for food to be cooked by the hospital will nevertheless be necessary.

Chapter 6
Teaching hospitals

Arrangements for the training of medical and other hospital staff and the administrative relationships between hospital and educational authorities, such as universities, may differ from one country to another. Most hospitals, however, have some teaching function and many general hospitals have training schools for nurses. Specialist staff, such as radiographers, may be trained in a variety of establishments. In Britain the term 'teaching hospital' has the specific meaning that whatever other training it may do, it is a place where medical students are taught to become physicians or surgeons. It is this category of hospital, with its highly integrated training, that is considered in this chapter.

Interdependent functions

Teaching hospitals combine three interdependent functions:

the treatment of the sick;

undergraduate and postgraduate education including nursing;

research.

Compared with many general hospitals teaching hospitals are larger in size, partly because of the number of beds and the range of specialities that are desirable to give students a wide experience, but principally on account of the additional accommodation needed for education and research. Their diagnostic and treatment departments also tend to be particularly specialised and to employ the most highly sophisticated equipment.

The teaching hospital is rightly regarded as a centre of excellence and an important centre of research. Because of these attributes there is a tendency for it to admit a relatively high proportion of patients who are suffering from 'interesting' or specially critical ailments, or who are of particular value from the point of view of research. This is inevitable in any primary, secondary and tertiary referral system.

The clinical experience offered by a teaching hospital may therefore not be entirely typical of the more common illnesses that the average young doctor is likely to encounter in general practice. For this reason, and although teaching hospitals may do their best to make their services available to the community in which they are situated, a period of the doctor's training is often in a general hospital. Where this is the policy it will have implications on the accommodation that is desirable in those establishments. The same consideration applies to the training of other medical, nursing and auxiliary staff.

The education of doctors is normally in two parts, undergraduate and postgraduate. The undergraduate stage usually lasts three years; the early part is mostly academic, or 'pre-clinical', dealing with the basic sciences and conducted in a medical school; the latter part is increasingly clinical, in which the student assists in the wards and some of the specialist departments, perhaps opting towards the end of the period for a particular specialism. In most countries the student then has a period of postgraduate training in hospitals, with some degree of responsibility, before he can practice as a doctor.

In the past the pre-clinical period has been separate, but where the standard of education of students entering medicine has been high the trend has been for this period to become less strictly academic and for students to be brought into contact with patients at a relatively early stage of their training.

The training of nurses is more closely integrated with the day-to-day work in the wards and other departments and is similar to a sandwich course. Practical work with patients, supervised by the sister and other senior nurses, alternates with periods of academic work in a school of nursing. The responsibility given to the student nurse in the hospital increases during the period of basic training, which normally lasts three years.

The hospital and the medical school

The accommodation provided in a teaching hospital differs from other hospitals in two principal ways. Space is needed for research, and also for a medical school for academic instruction. Both of these are to some degree separate from the hospital's ongoing function of caring for the sick. Space is also needed in the wards for clinical teaching, and in the past this has sometimes been interpreted as more room around the beds for large groups of students under instruction (the traditional teaching round).

Although such visitations still prevail, the student groups nowadays tend to be smaller and training is mainly done by discussion, demonstration and practical work in separate rooms which are now generally provided as an integral part of the ward. Thus the ancillary rooms necessary in the ward may be increased by seminar space for group discussions with the clinical staff and by clinical demonstration space to which a patient may be brought from the ward. Laboratories are also required for simple work by students on specimens from patients, and also rooms where students can read and write up their notes.

The teaching and demonstration function used to require the special design of some of the hospital's operating theatres, with galleries or other devices from which students could watch procedure. This requirement has today been largely superseded by colour film and closed circuit television, which have also immensely extended the range of demonstration in other medical fields.

Teaching accommodation not directly associated with clinical observation is provided in the medical school. In addition to the social and ancillary spaces generated by the needs of a large number of students it will include lecture theatres, seminar rooms, staff rooms, and the specialised plant of pre-clinical laboratories and dissecting rooms.

Pre-clinical teaching laboratories have traditionally been largely devoted to special subjects and have been specially designed for each purpose, such as biochemistry, physiology, histology, pharmacology, and anatomy. Each speciality has tended to retain its own territory and the students have moved in classes from one to another.

A more recent development that allows more intensive use of the accommodation and can be less divisive, less wasteful of space, and encourages a teaching unit more suitable for seminars, audio-visual aids and project work, is the smaller multi-discipline laboratory. Here most of the student's work can be done in one place (with the exception, probably, of anatomy, for which the centralised storage of cadavers

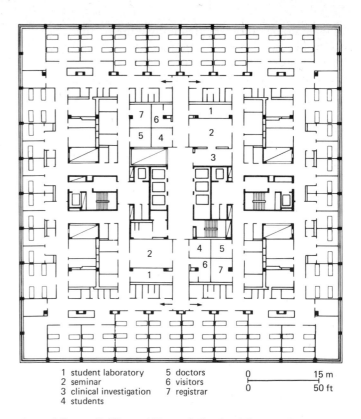

1 student laboratory	5 doctors
2 seminar	6 visitors
3 clinical investigation	7 registrar
4 students	

A ward floor at St Thomas' Hospital, London. There are four wards, each occupying one quarter of the perimeter. Clinical teaching accommodation in the form of student laboratories, seminar rooms and clinical investigation room is embedded in the middle of the building, with access both from within the wards and from the central lift lobby and corridor through which the wards are approached. Architects: Yorke Rosenberg Mardall

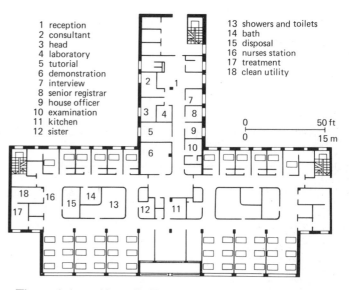

1 reception	13 showers and toilets
2 consultant	14 bath
3 head	15 disposal
4 laboratory	16 nurses station
5 tutorial	17 treatment
6 demonstration	18 clean utility
7 interview	
8 senior registrar	
9 house officer	
10 examination	
11 kitchen	
12 sister	

The ward plan at Ninewells Hospital. Two units of twenty-four beds are approached through a cross link which contains offices, laboratory, tutorial room and clinical demonstration room. Three day rooms and a balcony are shared between the units. Architects: Robert Matthew, Johnson-Marshall and Partners

is likely to be more practicable). In the multi-discipline laboratory the student has a place of his own, a home base, where he can do both his laboratory work and also his reading and writing.

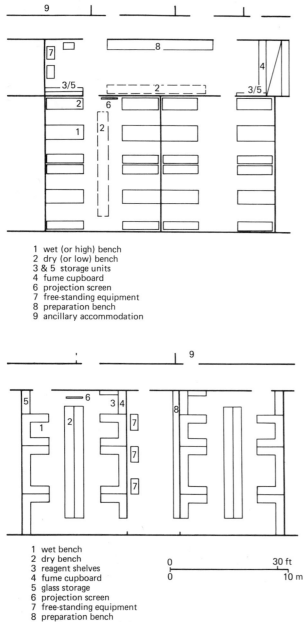

1 wet (or high) bench
2 dry (or low) bench
3 & 5 storage units
4 fume cupboard
6 projection screen
7 free-standing equipment
8 preparation bench
9 ancillary accommodation

1 wet bench
2 dry bench
3 reagent shelves
4 fume cupboard
5 glass storage
6 projection screen
7 free-standing equipment
8 preparation bench
9 ancillary accommodation

0   30 ft
0   10 m

Two basic layouts for multi-discipline laboratories in which the student has his own home base for wet and dry laboratory studies and for reading and written work. Each laboratory is for sixteen students and a pair share an interlab with preparation bench, freestanding equipment and fume cupboards if required. Architect: Audrey Williamson

Research

Laboratories for research present an entirely different picture from the large and relatively static teaching laboratories for instruction in particular specialities or the multi-discipline laboratories which provide bases in which students can study. Research projects may both come and go, ebb and flow, and throw up differing needs and differing sizes of teams. They need accommodation that will permit the flexibility that these changes demand.

Specialised spaces such as offices, preparation rooms, balance rooms, constant temperature rooms, autoclaves and workshops are likely to be necessary. It is desirable that most of the other working space should be standardised as far as possible in its planning module and in the servicing arrangements for electricity, water, piped gases, drainage and ventilation. Most laboratory work can function satisfactorily with movable benches and storage units located along or around pre-determined service lines or pedestals, arranged in undifferentiated bays.

The requirements of different research projects change and the boundaries between different specialities also tend to become less distinct. The planning of research laboratories should discourage the establishment of separate research empires with territorial rights and inviolable tailor-made rooms. The sharing of specialised facilities and the opportunity for expansion and contraction as research programmes demand should be encouraged.

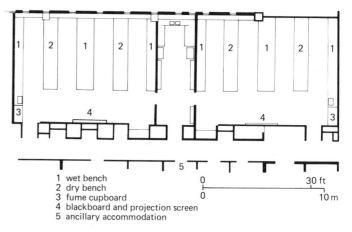

1 wet bench
2 dry bench
3 fume cupboard
4 blackboard and projection screen
5 ancillary accommodation

0   30 ft
0   10 m

Multi-discipline laboratories at Nottingham University Hospital and Medical School. Two laboratories share a preparation room and store. Wet benches with underbench lockers are serviced with gases and electricity and with water over drip cups; they alternate with lower tables for written work, serviced with electrical outlets for microscopes. Each laboratory has a sink and fume cupboard, and a chalkboard and projection screen on the back wall. Architects: Building Design Partnership

Initial design decisions can assist but not resolve the solution of this problem. However flexible the accommodation may be it is unlikely that it will be adequate for future requirements. Therefore, not only should the inevitability of change be recognised but the probability of growth should be anticipated and should be reflected in the siting of the accommodation.

Relationships

In some of the great teaching hospitals of the past the physical relationship between hospital, medical school and research accommodation has tended for various reasons to be less close than is now thought desirable. In part this has reflected the attitudes towards medical education at the time, and buildings have been developed on a succession of constricted sites which have offered little alternative. Apart from any psychological disadvantages, this separation can waste the time of staff in moving from one place to another and can sometimes tend to inhibit such movement if it can be avoided.

Although all the research accommodation usually needs to be planned as one unit sharing centralised facilities, it should when possible also be arranged so that it is near its associated hospital department. Although many of the research workers will be scientific rather than medical personnel, many of the medical specialists who lead the research projects will combine clinical work with research. If the medical school can also be closely associated with the hospital so much the better, for many of the hospital staff will also be involved with teaching. The more that the rigid division between the student's pre-clinical and clinical experience disappears and medical education is integrated with the work of the hospital the more valuable will these close physical relationships become.

A multi-discipline laboratory at Nottingham. Tables for dry work alternate with higher benches for wet work. Architects: Building Design Partnership

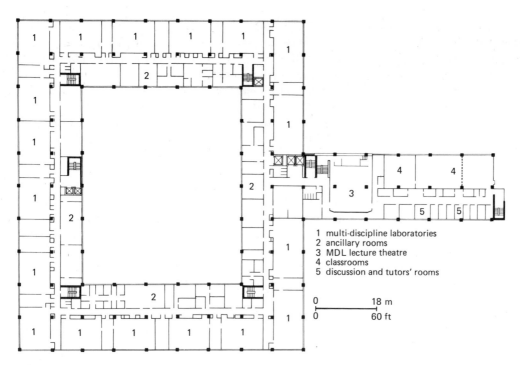

1 multi-discipline laboratories
2 ancillary rooms
3 MDL lecture theatre
4 classrooms
5 discussion and tutors' rooms

0   18 m
0   60 ft

*A floor of multi-discipline laboratories and associated rooms,
including a large lecture theatre, in the medical school block at
Nottingham. The block has five main levels, with an animal house on
the roof. The lowest level contains library, lecture theatres and
workshops; the second seminar rooms, offices, common rooms,
professors' and readers' laboratories; the third multi-discipline
laboratories and ancillary rooms; the fourth professors', lecturers' and
teaching laboratories and film and medical artists; and the fifth
dissecting laboratories, specialist professors', readers' and lecturers'
laboratories, and laboratories for 3rd and Final Year honours. The
link block is on four levels and houses the nurses' training school.
Architects: Building Design Partnership*

Comparative examples

An example of a newly designed teaching hospital
which made a determined attempt at close integration
of the clinical, teaching and research functions was the
new Charing Cross Hospital in London. Planned on a
relatively restricted site in an urban area the ward
block took the shape of a multi-storey cruciform in
which one wing of the cross contained research,
teaching laboratories and clinical teaching space, and
the other three wings were occupied by beds.

A later London example, also on a restricted site
but part of the phased redevelopment of an existing
hospital, is to be seen at St. Thomas' Hospital. Here
clinical investigation rooms, seminar rooms and clinical laboratories for student work are embedded with
the other ward ancillaries in the core of a rectangular
multi-storey block, and the beds and day spaces

occupy the whole of the perimeter. Laboratories
occupy some of the lower floors of this ward block and
a research institute shares with diagnostic and treatment, operating and outpatients departments an
adjacent building linked closely to it below the level of
the wards.

An entirely different type of solution, impossible on
the urban sites of the two previous examples, is the
Ninewells Hospital at Dundee in Scotland. With more
space to spread, low-rise buildings of not more than
three storeys were practicable. The three elements –
the wards, the paraclinical laboratories and lecture
theatres, and the pre-clinical laboratories and library
– are disposed in parallel lines with cross-links
between them. There is also a fourth element, medical
physics, on a line which is most remote from the wards.

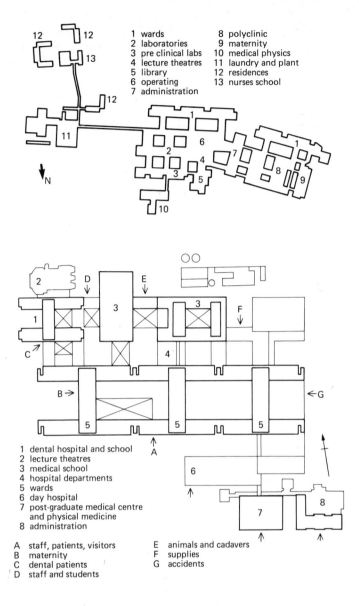

1 wards
2 laboratories
3 pre clinical labs
4 lecture theatres
5 library
6 operating
7 administration
8 polyclinic
9 maternity
10 medical physics
11 laundry and plant
12 residences
13 nurses school

Ninewells Hospital and Medical School, Dundee; an 865 bed hospital and medical school for 400 students. There are in principle three parallel lines of accommodation, with cross links. The wards, which include clinical teaching rooms, are situated on the south face; there is then a line of paraclinical laboratories, theatres and diagnostic departments. On the north are the preclinical laboratories, lecture theatres and medical library. Operating theatres and administration are at the fulcrum. Medical physics, the department least associated with the wards, is in a separate building on the extreme north. To the east the laundry, plant, nurses' training school and residences leave space for expansion of the main building.

1 dental hospital and school
2 lecture theatres
3 medical school
4 hospital departments
5 wards
6 day hospital
7 post-graduate medical centre and physical medicine
8 administration

A staff, patients, visitors
B maternity
C dental patients
D staff and students
E animals and cadavers
F supplies
G accidents

Development plan for the Royal Victoria Infirmary and Medical School, Newcastle upon Tyne. There are three parallel lines of accommodation with cross-links. On the north are the medical school, lecture theatres and dental school; hospital departments are in the centre and wards on the south face. The day hospital, physical medicine and post-graduate medical centre extend to the south, linked to an existing administrative building. Architects: Robert Matthew, Johnson-Marshall and Partners

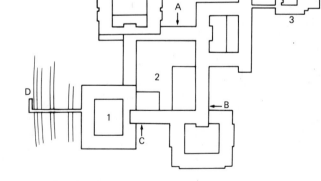

A main entrance
B service entrance
C nurses training school
D bridge to University

1 medical school and medical sciences
2 diagnosis and treatment
3 works department

Nottingham University Hospital and Medical School provides 1400 beds in three large quadrangular blocks; accommodation for the medical school and medical sciences is in the fourth. The blocks are linked by a ring system of corridors; one of these links contains the nurses' training school. Diagnostic and treatment departments are in the central area. A bridge over a main roadconnects the medical school with the university campus. Architects: Building Design Partnership

Compared with the restraints imposed by a condensed multi-storey arrangement this pattern clearly has the advantage of providing some opportunity for future growth by the lateral extension of any of the elements. Here again the T-shaped wards show the close juxtaposition of clinical teaching accommodation and patients, with tutorial and demonstration rooms in the area through which the beds are approached.

A similar gradation from pre-clinical to clinical and community departments, with cross links, is seen in the plan for the Royal Victoria Infirmary at Newcastle. Here the parallel lines of accommodation contain firstly the medical school and dental hospital and school; secondly the main hospital departments, and thirdly the wards, with physical medicine and the day hospital in a further unit beyond the wards.

The University Hospital and Medical School at Nottingham demonstrates another type of solution to the close integration of pre-clinical and clinical work. Four blocks, each forming a hollow rectangle, are linked by a larger square containing a corridor ring, of which one side is largely occupied by the Nurses' Training School. Within the ring is a central area of diagnostic, treatment and service departments. Three of the hollow blocks contain wards and the fourth is the Medical School, one of whose six floors is entirely occupied by multi-discipline laboratories and their ancillary accommodation.

Chapter 7
Psychiatric services

Mental illness can afflict people of any nationality, culture or background, and of any age or intellectual capacity. It can incapacitate them as seriously as many other identifiable diseases. It is not, as is sometimes popularly supposed, essentially a product of the stressful developed world. A World Health Organisation expert committee on mental health estimated in 1974 that in the developing countries over 40 million men, women and children were suffering from serious untreated mental disorder.

However it is only relatively recently that a substantial body of opinion has attempted to explain this form of illness. Although its mechanisms are still imperfectly understood and it is not always possible to effect a cure or to remove the factors that cause it, psychiatry, a newcomer to medical science, has reached a stage at which the majority of cases will respond to treatment.

Psychiatry today is in a period of change more rapid than conventional medicine, not only in its methods of treatment but more fundamentally in its social objectives. In the relatively recent past people whose behaviour was bizarre, unacceptable or dangerous were offered asylum or had asylum forced upon them in order to withdraw them from a society inconvenienced by their activities.

The aim today can perhaps best be characterised by the objective of modifying their patterns of living and their ability to adjust to other people so that they can learn to return, perhaps by degrees, to 'normal' life. Instead of being regarded as unreliably peculiar the treatment of mental illness is becoming increasingly integrated with general medicine in the 'normal' hospital and with the associated health and social services.

Psychiatric treatment is increasingly available on a voluntary basis rather than as a sequel to compulsory detention. Its range of care has also extended widely. Severe mental disorder was formerly its principal preoccupation but today, besides its concern with the ability of people to cope with the strains and stresses of everyday living, it embraces personality disorders, alcoholism and drug addiction, delinquency and emotionally disturbed children and adolescents.

Old methods of treatment

The 19th century conception of care for the 'mad' is epitomised by the huge and forbidding mental hospital or asylum. In these buildings patients were confined in the atmosphere of a prison, preferably far away from any large centre of population, so that normal society could go its own way protected from their vagaries and violence. Little if any distinction was made between the mentally ill and the mentally handicapped. In these institutions the inmates could be regarded as an isolated and self-contained community safely removed from the world to which it was unlikely that they would return.

In a WHO paper of 1959, '*Psychiatric Services and Architecture*', there is a description of the impact that the vast old mental hospital would have on the patient. It bears repeating not only because it emphasises what should be avoided but also because by implication the antithesis is so clear.

'It is common for the hospital to be approached by a stately drive which culminates in a direct approach to the centre of an enormous block of buildings . . . . . Such buildings make the visitor feel small, powerless, and insignificant. The effect on the patient is to increase any tendency he may have to run away, to destroy this frightening object or such parts of it as he can, or to retreat into inert submission.

Once inside the door . . . . . the patient is usually taken from an entrance hall to a records department where his documents will be examined by a member of the lay staff. After this he will be escorted down long corridors where he will see numbers of patients sitting or walking aimlessly, perhaps exhibiting gross evidence of desocialization and eccentricity. He may then arrive at an admission unit, where he will be examined by a doctor before being taken to yet another unit which will be his ward for initial observation and treatment. He will then be put to bed and left to observe his surroundings. He will see the many beds, all alike, and the absence of other furnishings, the walls of dull, uniform institution buff or brown, and the windows small, high, barred and often dirty. There will be evidence of locks and he will hear the keys of his attendants. The ward will have a stale smell and often provide evidence of the inadequacy of the sanitary arrangements. He will also find within the ward no privacy, or opportunity to create it. He will be forced to perform even the most private activities where he can be seen both by other patients and the staff. Within a crowd of such patients there will be no opportunity to form friendships with a small group, or to feel any drive to identify himself with those around him. Within this environment our patient feels no encouragement to develop human relationships, and he will see that his life is without purpose. Any tendency to aggressive behaviour caused by his illness will be reinforced by the architecture and by the regime which the design of the building tends to perpetuate.'

Institutions like the above still exist and, in some parts of the world, mental patients are still kept chained in conditions of mediaeval squalor, shunned by their relatives and friends. But with the spread of communications and education, the growth of industry and urbanisation and the changes in traditional communities and beliefs it seems inevitable that mental illness, like other forms of sickness, will come to be regarded everywhere as something that demands and will respond to a different form of treatment. However constituted the health service will have to provide for its alleviation.

Treatment today

There are still occasions when physical confinement of the mentally ill is necessary but this is not the general rule. New approaches to treatment have made it possible to guide most of the mentally ill back to normal life. Since the 1950s the development of drugs has not only removed some of the need for physical restraint but has enabled doctors and nurses to maintain human contact with a patient who would otherwise have repudiated any effort of assistance.

In some countries the growth of social services in the community has helped in the work of readjustment, rehabilitation and support that the patient needs after responding to treatment and re-entering society. The social services also have begun to provide the type of care than can ameliorate and sometimes avoid the factors that seem to contribute to this form of illness.

Treatment is based increasingly on out-patient clinics, day hospitals and various types of community care and less on the admission of patients to residential care in a hospital. It takes many different forms, or combinations of forms, including physical treatments such as drugs or electro-convulsive therapy (ECT), and various techniques of socially interactive therapy. The latter are possibly the most important in their bearing on the design of the accommodation. From 'talking' treatment on a one-to-one basis in a comfortable consulting room they may range through small discussion groups to larger ones of a dozen or more. It may offer encouragement for participation in a variety of everyday activities that can contribute to the patient's self-reliance and readjustment to society.

Psychiatrists differ in their approaches however; some use drugs and electro-convulsive therapy as their main avenue, others use 'talking' therapies. Still others may use 'role playing' methods in which rehabilitation is based on training in social skills and work skills.

The old type of mental institution, relying upon confinement behind locked doors and formidable boundary walls, did not need many people to run it. Staff did not require a particularly high degree of training, for they were custodians rather than nurses. In most establishments caring for mental illness today a higher ratio of staff to patients is usual; a variety of skills is available and an entirely different emphasis needs to be placed on the nature and character of the buildings. Whereas the old institution deliberately imparted a sense of withdrawal and physical restraint imposed by authority the new will try to avoid too overt a feeling of segregation from society. It will aim to foster an atmosphere of security of a very different sort – as normal and as domestic as is practicable within an establishment that in scale is usually larger than domestic – and in which supervision, although necessary, will be incidental to the other activities in which the staff are engaged with the patients.

Varieties of care

Buildings for the mentally ill are for most patients 'staging posts' where they can be encouraged to find their way back to normal patterns of everyday life and to their families, friends and occupations. Unlike short stay patients in a surgical ward, for example, who may often be discharged soon after treatment, their process of readjustment is likely to be much slower.

Thus to a greater extent than other buildings for health care, this type of building must provide opportunities and encouragement for social and occupational activities that can assist the patient's progress towards the goal of 'normal' life. The main object is to give physical and psychological shelter; the strictly clinical facilities are relatively few. Most patients are fully ambulant and the bed is much less the focus of attention than in medicine or surgery, for only a small minority of patients need that type of care and then only for short periods.

But even with the most modern psychiatric care there will remain a small proportion of patients who need more or less permanent support in a hospital environment. For example, there are some patients with degenerative and irreversible mental symptoms associated with old age, and some who are continuously behaviourally disturbed or persistently violent. These patients must be treated in conditions of physical security. There are some with dangerous or criminal propensities for whom a particularly high degree of security is necessary.

Patients without families or friends to whom they can go after discharge or who, although they have homes to return to, may not be able to sustain the strain of normal society or employment without further support, may need continued partial psychiatric care. These patients may be well enough to find a place in society during the working day but may need to return to the protection of a hospital for the night. Alternatively, they may need to spend part of the day at an institution and return to their homes in the evenings to sleep. Whatever the pattern it is generally accepted that the aim must be to avoid arrangements whereby they are encouraged to depend on constant in-patient care and become institutionalised and chronically sick.

It will be seen from the preceding paragraphs that mental illness demands several varieties of care and that there are many gradations between one degree of care and another. Compared with acute medical and surgical cases the course of sickness and cure is less mechanical and proceeds in less of a straight line. It may also be much slower. Thus the types of accommodation that are needed are more varied and less specific, and because of the state of knowledge can be regarded as considerably more experimental.

Because mental illness seems to be caused by personal stresses arising from the patient's relation to the family or to society the manner of treatment and the appropriate institution (if indeed an institution is appropriate at all) may vary greatly from one culture to another to a much greater extent than does the short stay hospital.

Social customs and religious beliefs influence, and may determine, not only the way in which mental illness can best be tackled but also the readiness of sufferers to seek help. Thus generalisations, which are dangerous enough in any discussion of health facilities

that embraces both the developing and developed world, are doubly so in the field of psychiatric services. The range of facilities will clearly differ from one country to another. However, in much of the developed world where the birth rate is more or less static, the population is ageing and health services are fairly readily available, there will be an increasing need for facilities which care for the elderly and the geriatric.

In the developing world where the population is continuing to expand and there is a higher proportion of young people, the emphasis is more likely to be on children and adolescents. The range will also depend on the extent to which other supportive facilities have been established in the community. This will have a considerable influence on the need for in-patient care as distinct from out-patient or day-patient partial care supplemented by various forms of community care.

It is now usually accepted that community care is the more desirable approach, both for its preventive advantages and for the avoidance of chronic institutionalisation. Although there must still be a place for the specialist mental hospital, the majority of cases are better treated in other forms of institution in which the patient is withdrawn as little as possible, or for only brief periods, from the society to which his cure is attempting to re-adapt him.

The general hospital

Over the past few decades there has been an increasing tendency in western countries for the psychiatric treatment of adults (as distinct from children and the geriatric) to be integrated with the general hospital where this is possible. Apart from other advantages this can help to reduce the unfortunate social stigma that is still often associated with mental illness.

Thus many general hospitals include emergency clinics for walk-in patients, in-patient psychiatric wards, out-patient psychiatric clinics, and day hospital facilities for rehabilitation and occupational therapy. In large district general hospitals in the UK these facilities may constitute a separate large department with upwards of sixty in-patient beds. However, experience has shown that such units cannot satisfactorily deal with all patients in need of psychiatric services, such as those whose behaviour is very bizarre or violent, or those whose illness is chronic.

Emergency clinics for walk-in patients in the general hospital are only likely to be necessary in some urban areas. Ideally they should perhaps be separate from the accident and emergency department, whose work in dealing with casualties may otherwise be disrupted. But, in general, the accident and emergency staff are likely to have to cover this service with the help of a psychiatrist.

If separate, the emergency clinic should not be in an isolated location but close to a department which is well staffed at all times so that if necessary it can be called upon to help deal with sudden aggressive emergencies. The accommodation needed is of the simplest: a manned reception point, some waiting space, and some interview rooms.

Some walk-in cases may be violent or suicidal, and at least one of the interview rooms should be arranged with this in mind. It should be furnished so that the fittings cannot readily be damaged and, in addition, do not offer the patient the opportunity of damaging himself. The same considerations apply to some degree to all this accommodation.

Out-patient clinics may well form part of the hospital's general out-patient department, or be associated with it. Psychiatric out-patients can share the waiting areas, will use the hospital pharmacy, and may need access to other facilities which are used by the department. Normal consulting rooms for doctors, psychologists and other professionals will be needed, but larger and more specialised rooms may be required for group therapy. These should be capable of seating about twelve patients and staff informally and equipped with a one-way screen between the group room and an adjacent room from which behaviour can be observed, with facilities for microphones and recorders.

Wards for in-patients usually contain between twenty and thirty beds. In the UK thirty is favoured as the optimum and two wards of this size as probably the minimum viable for a district general hospital. Psychiatric wards usually accommodate both men and women, with separate sleeping arrangements for the sexes. As in all other accommodation for psychiatric patients, the planning should aim to help observation through interaction between staff and patients rather than rely on strict custodial care.

Three degrees of care can be identified, according to the degree of the patient's dependence on nursing, and the sub-division and arrangement of the ward can reflect this. These degrees may be termed High Dependency, Intermediate, and Minimum (or Low) Dependency.
They may be reflected both in the planning of the ward and in the use which the patients can make of other parts of the ward, such as day spaces, and of the facilities which the hospital provides outside the ward.

Some High Dependency patients may be on their beds for much of the time. They may be seriously disturbed or heavily sedated, and a few may need nursing in bed. They should be accommodated in single rooms close to the staff base; their doors should be capable of being opened outwards, for they may be barricaded by the patient from within. Observation panels, windows, mirrors, etc should be of toughened or splinterproof material. A washbasin will probably be provided, but it should be indestructible.

An assisted bath, a shower and a toilet should be closely accessible from this group of rooms, for it is tedious for staff and upsetting for other patients if the highly disturbed have to be escorted along corridors to reach them. Five single rooms of this nature may be a reasonable complement for a thirty bed ward, two of them capable of taking a baby's cot at the side of the mother's bed.

The Intermediate category of patient may be ambulant some of the time and perhaps dressed. They may be wandering around the ward but cannot safely be allowed to do so unless they can be kept under observation. Some of them may be encouraged to use the day areas within the ward or to sit in the corridors (particularly if these have been designed with this in mind).

These patients are progressing and although some of them may spend part of the day on their beds they do not need single rooms and should not be encouraged to want them. Perhaps two rooms of about five beds, each including a little day space (about the equivalent of a six-bed room) can help to encourage group relationships at this stage of illness. They should be near the staff base and should preferably have toilets adjacent.

Minimum or Low Dependency patients are those who have progressed to the stage at which most of them can participate in group therapy activities or make use of the occupational therapy and other facilities that the hospital provides. They will be fully ambulant and dressed, and for much of the day many of them may not be in the ward but in the Day Hospital, mixing and taking part in activities with the day patients.

On the ward they can profit from more individualised bed spaces than can the Intermediate category. They may well be in five-bed rooms which can be flexibly sub-divided into personal corners and cubicles by screens and storage furniture. In a thirty-bed ward about half the beds might be provided in this manner.

The ward should provide bed areas, the sanitary and utility accommodation and staff base (which should include a treatment room with particularly secure storage for drugs). In addition there should be a ward office and one or more rooms in which doctors and others can interview patients and their relatives, a beverage pantry to which patients have access, and some variety of patients' day spaces.

As a minimum, these day spaces should include an

active area and a quieter one capable of being separated from it, and should provide some opportunity for occupational therapy. They may be used as a dining area by patients who cannot leave the ward; alternatively there may be advantages if a larger dining area can be shared by more than one ward. At times the day areas may be used for group meetings of patients and staff and a degree of flexibility can be useful for purposes such as this. In addition there should be somewhere for patients to wash and dry their own clothes and a room for hairwashing and hairdressing.

This type of psychiatric ward may not, however, be able to deal with all patients admitted to the hospital. There are likely to be some who are so disturbed and disruptive that they cannot be treated alongside other patients while they are in this condition. For these patients an annexe of about ten beds may be valuable, separate from the wards but with easy access for staff from one of them.

It will be necessary to be able to lock up the annexe, for security will be of particular importance, but the atmosphere should remain as domestic as possible in the circumstances. At a reduced scale it will need much the same ancillary and day accommodation as the normal ward, including a small staff base. British practice for a unit of ten beds in this category tends to be to provide six in single rooms and the remainder in one multi-bed room.

The day hospital

The purpose of the day hospital is to provide some clinical facilities, but principally occupational, recreational and social accommodation for day patients who are living in the community and for those in-patients who are well enough to visit it from the psychiatric wards. It is entered by patients separately from other parts of the hospital and may usefully be in

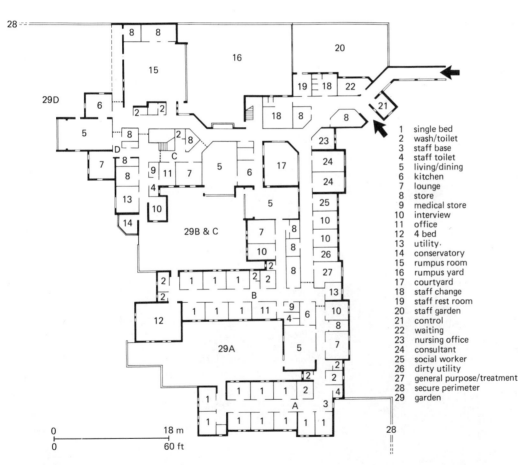

1 single bed
2 wash/toilet
3 staff base
4 staff toilet
5 living/dining
6 kitchen
7 lounge
8 store
9 medical store
10 interview
11 office
12 4 bed
13 utility
14 conservatory
15 rumpus room
16 rumpus yard
17 courtyard
18 staff change
19 staff rest room
20 staff garden
21 control
22 waiting
23 nursing office
24 consultant
25 social worker
26 dirty utility
27 general purpose/treatment
28 secure perimeter
29 garden

A medium-secure residential unit for forty patients, linked to Frierne mental hospital, Middlesex. It is arranged in four residential 'houses' of ten patients. Each house has its own day and dining spaces, and its internal circulation is separate from the main access corridor. The four houses permit the unit to operate on the basis of progressive patient care, the high dependency patients being in house A. Bedrooms for houses C and D are on an upper floor. All houses open on to garden areas with a secure perimeter. The only access to the unit is past the control room in the link with the main hospital. Architects: Hutchinson Locke and Monk

Preliminary model for one of several medium-secure inpatient clinics to be built in the grounds of existing mental hospitals in the South East Thames region. They are intended to provide intermediate facilities for mentally disordered patients who are not so ill that they should be in a special maximum security hospital but are nevertheless too disruptive for the ordinary wards of a psychiatric hospital. The patients' length of stay will vary but will rarely be more than 18 months.

The central block from which the three wings radiate contains dining and living space, overlooked by a nurses' station. From this smaller rooms for various activities are approached. There are ten beds in the wing in the foreground and five in that on the right. Staff accommodation is in the wing on the left. The bedroom wings and central block open on to a secure garden on the opposite side of the building from the access road. Architects: Hutchinson Locke and Monk. (Photo: Sam Lambert)

Preliminary model for a central thirty place medium-secure unit in the grounds of Bethlem Royal Hospital, Kent, to which the clinics are related. Three wings each contain 10 single bedrooms. The fourth wing, at the main entrance, houses boilers and a separate unit for electro-encephalography (EEG). Communal facilities are in the central courtyard building, which has an upper floor of staff accommodation. There are three secure gardens. Architects: Hutchinson Locke and Monk. (Photo: Sam Lambert)

an independent building. It should be linked to the main hospital and if possible to the out-patients' department, for some psychiatric day patients may make use of the hospitals' occupational therapy and gymnasium facilities.

The bulk of the accommodation will provide spaces for everyday activities such as housekeeping, the preparation and cooking of food, dressmaking, laundering, ironing and child care. There should also

be accommodation for occupational activities such as woodwork, metalwork, pottery, weaving, painting, music, typing, according to the cultures of the country or district in which it is situated.

There will be a central dining area for some of the day patients and for those in-patients who can leave the wards, and space for concerts, films, dancing and parties or assemblies, perhaps by multiple use of the dining area. The rest of the accommodation will be made up of offices and cloakrooms for nursing, social work, domestic and administrative staff, consulting and interview rooms, and group therapy rooms, some of which may need one way screens for observation from an adjoining room.

Facilities for electro-convulsive therapy (ECT) may be required in the psychiatric unit and may possibly be sited in the Day Hospital. Some psychiatrists use

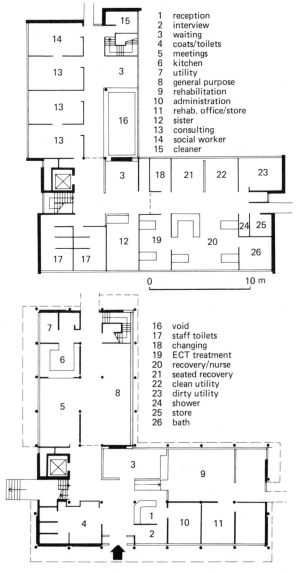

1	reception
2	interview
3	waiting
4	coats/toilets
5	meetings
6	kitchen
7	utility
8	general purpose
9	rehabilitation
10	administration
11	rehab. office/store
12	sister
13	consulting
14	social worker
15	cleaner
16	void
17	staff toilets
18	changing
19	ECT treatment
20	recovery/nurse
21	seated recovery
22	clean utility
23	dirty utility
24	shower
25	store
26	bath

A psychiatric day hospital at Evesham. It is the first phase of a new Avonside general hospital and will remain a separate unit at the extremity of later hospital development along a linear hospital street. Rehabilitation and social areas are off the main entrance downstairs; upstairs there are consulting rooms and a suite for electro-convulsive therapy and recovery. Waiting spaces are slightly withdrawn into partially screened alcoves. A void over part of the social area helps to give a sense of unity to the two levels. Architects: Derek Stow and Partners

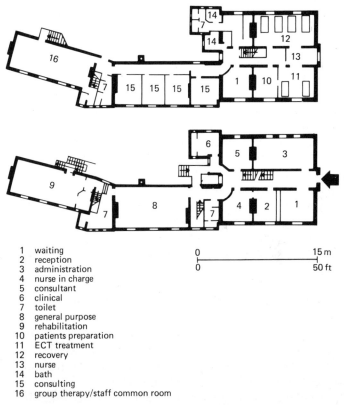

1	waiting
2	reception
3	administration
4	nurse in charge
5	consultant
6	clinical
7	toilet
8	general purpose
9	rehabilitation
10	patients preparation
11	ECT treatment
12	recovery
13	nurse
14	bath
15	consulting
16	group therapy/staff common room

The conversion of an old building into a psychiatric day centre at Malvern, Worcs. The main entrance is from the road at the north end; there are gardens on the east side and car parking on the west. Nearly all the existing walls of the building have been used and only a few new openings have been made or partitions demolished. On the ground floor the general purpose room (the main social area) leads through to a light rehabilitation workshop. Upstairs are consulting rooms and electro-convulsive therapy and recovery, and a group therapy room which is also used as a staff common room. A lower ground floor, approached from the main entrance hall, accommodates dining room and kitchen. There is a separate caretaker's flat below the rehabilitation workshop. Architects: Derek Stow and Partners

this form of treatment more than others. When it is required, the ECT suite is likely to comprise a small waiting space for perhaps half a dozen patients, a sound-proofed treatment room in which the patient is anaesthetised and the treatment administered, with services for resuscitation in case of emergency, and a recovery room, with oxygen and suction, divided into two areas for anaesthetised patients on trolleys or couches and for those sufficiently recovered to be able to sit in chairs and rest. The recovery room needs a pantry nearby for the preparation of tea or coffee.

In accommodation for the mentally ill it is easier than in most parts of the hospital for designers to achieve a comfortable and reassuring domestic atmosphere. Many of the constraints imposed by equipment and sterility are absent and most of the floorings and furnishings can be soft. But there are likely to be problems arising from the sheer size of the building or department which militate against domesticity.

Although it is important for confused and disorientated patients that planning should be lucid and routes easy to follow, long corridors can be intimidating, however decorated or adorned, particularly if they are internal and offer no prospect of the world outside. They can, however, be planned so that they provide opportunities for social meeting or withdrawal, with alcoves or bays where it is inviting to sit down. In some cases they can be combined with day areas.

There are also likely to be problems arising from the demands of security and safety; it should not be easy for patients to escape without being noticed or for those with suicidal tendencies to find opportunities of indulging them. There must be adequate provision for escape in case of fire (and some patients may be prone to setting things alight) but the escape routes may need to be monitored, perhaps electrically. All windows accessible to patients, particularly on upper floors, should be restricted in the amount they can be opened.

Great ingenuity may be exercised in overcoming these constraints and the use of toughened glass or plastic may be advisable in some areas. Furniture and fittings can also be vulnerable and may provide a patient with something with which to damage himself or other people. Some furniture, such as seating in alcoves, may of course be fixed.

Design should offer patients the opportunity of going outdoors. This presents few problems in the case of the day hospital, where space should be provided for sitting out, for strolling and for games; in some localities there may with advantage be facilities for gardening and horticulture. Such outdoor areas are usually best reached from the dining and social areas, from occupational therapy and from the nursery, if there is one.

Where security is of importance care needs to be taken that outdoor areas help the staff to contain patients without creating the impression that they are locked in. High wire fences are not the only answer; properly planted walled gardens or courtyards are better, particularly in single-storey buildings. Dense hedges may be equally effective provided these are properly situated in relation to the building so that staff can exercise unobtrusive supervision.

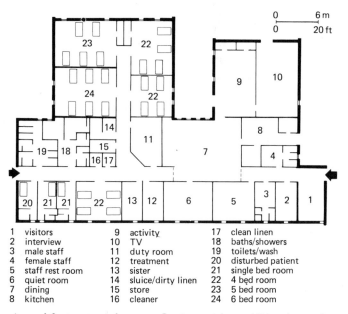

1	visitors	9	activity	17	clean linen
2	interview	10	TV	18	baths/showers
3	male staff	11	duty room	19	toilets/wash
4	female staff	12	treatment	20	disturbed patient
5	staff rest room	13	sister	21	single bed room
6	quiet room	14	sluice/dirty linen	22	4 bed room
7	dining	15	store	23	5 bed room
8	kitchen	16	cleaner	24	6 bed room

A ward for twenty-eight men at Jumiera, with an additional room for a disturbed patient. A mix of one, two, four, five and six bed arrangements are centred on the duty room, and there is a variety of social rooms for dining, quiet and noisier activities and television. A visitors' space and interview room are arranged off a separate entrance lobby

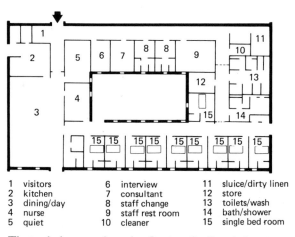

1	visitors	6	interview	11	sluice/dirty linen
2	kitchen	7	consultant	12	store
3	dining/day	8	staff change	13	toilets/wash
4	nurse	9	staff rest room	14	bath/shower
5	quiet	10	cleaner	15	single bed room

The ten-bed protected ward at Jumiera for disturbed patients who need to be segregated. All bedrooms are single and have their own toilets. All the beds are approached from a corridor which can be separated from the rest of the accommodation, but the nurses' room communicated with bedrooms and day space

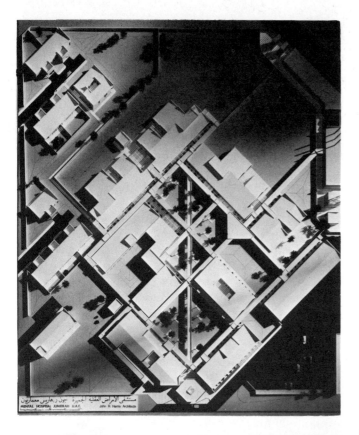

A mental hospital at Jumiera, United Arab Emirates; a single storey building with beds for 111 inpatients. The entrance gatehouse is at the bottom of the picture; administration, kitchen and laundry occupy the south side of the rectangle; separate wards for ten children and thirty-five women are on the east side, and two twenty-eight bed wards for men on the north. Next to the gatehouse, on the west side, is the social centre, which leads through to the treatment and therapy complex that occupies a quarter of the centre of the rectangle and is accessible to outpatients. The other unit within the rectangle is a protected ward for ten patients who need segregation; this has a small secure internal courtyard. Covered walkways subdivide the centre of the hospital into garden courts. Housing for staff and servants lies outside the hospital to the north and west. The buildings for plant on the east leave space for the addition of further men's and women's wards. Architect: John R. Harris. (Photo: Henk Snoek/Crispin Boyle)

The entrance gatehouse at Jumiera is in the foreground on the right, with the social centre on the left. (Photo: Henk Snoek/Crispin Boyle)

Mental hospitals

Psychiatric in-patient facilities in the general hospital are primarily suitable for short-stay patients. In time it may be possible to house long-stay patients in hospital hostels or in hostel wards, but even so there will almost certainly remain a need for the specialist mental hospital, particularly if adequate community based services are lacking.

Mental hospitals are frequently situated away from town or city centres and are not physically associated with the general hospital. If possible they should be developed at relatively low density in buildings of domestic scale in adequate grounds; 400 beds should probably be considered the absolute maximum, although regrettably there are still old institutions of nearly four times this size.

Whereas in the general hospital the relationships between different departments induce close communications and compactness of planning, there is no reason why a mental hospital should be arranged as a single building. Indeed if the site is adequate there are many advantages in planning it as a collection of separate and dissimilar buildings more analogous to a loosely spaced village. These could be connected in some places by covered ways if the climate justifies it. This arrangement can help to avoid some of the dangers of institutionalisation and with some activities can foster the feeling that it is natural to go out for work or entertainment or to meet with other people.

The elements of accommodation will be similar in function to those in the general hospital, but not identical. Admission wards will provide the same facilities but may have to cope with more patients in an acute stage of illness and are likely to justify a higher degree of security. The long-stay living accommodation may well take a form more akin to separate houses or hostels where a patient can have his own territory. This may be no more than the equivalent of a cubicle for keeping personal belongings in safety and perhaps creating a congenial atmosphere even if it is only his own muddle.

The size of each house or hostel should be the smallest that is compatible with the needs of the patient for privacy and society, and the availability of staff. Cooking may well have to be centralised but the more that dining can be broken down into smaller units the better. Comfortable sitting room or lounge spaces for reading or watching TV will be needed in each living unit. Other social activities may well take place in a separate community centre having facilities for indoor games and sports, entertainments, cafe refreshments and so on.

Working activities may extend from normal occupational therapy to rehabilitation workshops, where suitable contract work for local business can be undertaken in sheltered conditions under expert guidance. This may even provide some income for the patients.

Other facilities for the mentally ill

The day hospital, the general hospital and the mental hospital are likely to be able to cater for only a proportion of patients. For many people these establishments will not be near enough at hand and may not in any case provide the right environment. Something more local and smaller in scale may be desirable, even when the support of local medical practitioners, health centres and the social services are available.

There have been some programmes, notably in the USA but also elsewhere, that aim to fill this gap by providing community based mental health centres with facilities for diagnosis, therapy, rehabilitation and social activity. Residential accommodation is sometimes provided, linked to the hospital service but not psychologically associated with it. Generally these units are in urban areas and are in physically independent buildings whose character is as far as possible the reverse of clinical.

Some centres have been housed in converted domestic buildings; others have been newly constructed for their purpose. They may provide beds or may be run in conjunction with separate sheltered residential accommodation in ordinary houses in the

The community centre at Bethlem Royal Hospital, Beckenham, Kent. Two parallel blocks two storeys high are linked together in the middle. One contains light occupational therapy, education, and rooms for social purposes and light refreshments; the other has a small swimming pool and a general purpose hall for theatre, cinema and dances. Architects: Architects' Co-Partnership

neighbourhood, or they may be based on a combination of both.

The function and facilities of such centres will vary according to the needs of the district in which they are located. Primarily they are likely to aim at providing comprehensive after-care and rehabilitation for men and women who have been discharged from psychiatric hospitals, to help them to readjust to normal community living. This may be combined with care for referred patients for whom the only alternative, and a less suitable one, would be admission to hospital.

Unavoidably they may have on occasions to deal with walk-in cases, even if only temporarily. Some of them can be called Day Centres, others might more appropriately be called Day and Night Centres. They are truly half-way houses. They are essentially community buildings and are most likely to be acceptable in the community if they are part of it and if externally they look as if they belong to it. Internally their design needs to foster a feeling of friendliness, of a club in which patients and staff are living together; it needs also to encourage social encounters as much as possible and an awareness of all the activities that are going on in the place.

The design will tend towards compactness, but there may be conflicts between this and the needs of security and even of segregation. This is particularly the case if the centre provides not only residential accommodation but also some normal in-patient beds and thus may at times have to deal with badly disturbed people.

Accommodation is likely to include an entrance hall, welcoming and habitable in character but supervised; perhaps the entrance lounge of a small hotel is the best analogy. There will be rooms for the

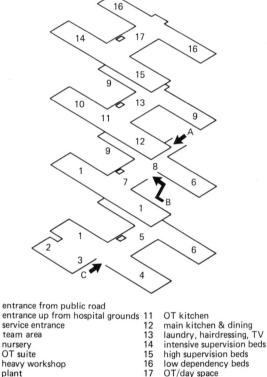

A entrance from public road
B entrance up from hospital grounds
C service entrance
1 team area
2 nursery
3 OT suite
4 heavy workshop
5 plant
6 offices
7 waiting & coffee stall
8 reception
9 research
10 group room, classroom, library
11 OT kitchen
12 main kitchen & dining
13 laundry, hairdressing, TV
14 intensive supervision beds
15 high supervision beds
16 low dependency beds
17 OT/day space

Exploded view showing the four storey arrangement of a psychiatric centre at the Maudsley Hospital to serve the Camberwell district. Situated in an urban area it combines day care for 111 patients with residential care for thirty-four. Although intended principally for day patients it is possible for some patients to occupy a bed for a period without interrupting the continuity of care by admission to a mental hospital or a psychiatric ward elsewhere. Beds are on the top floor and social facilities on the floor below; on the two lower floors there are three distinct team areas, each for about 36 patients in groups of 13. Suites for light and heavy occupational therapy are at ground level. Parts of the building provide offices for a Medical Research Council Unit. There is a difference in level of one storey between the hospital grounds and the public road. Architects: Architects' Co-Partnership

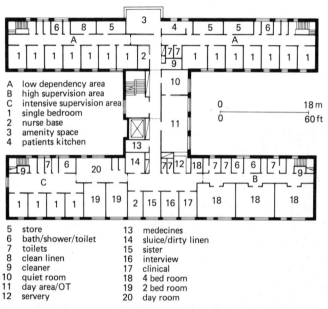

A low dependency area
B high supervision area
C intensive supervision area
1 single bedroom
2 nurse base
3 amenity space
4 patients kitchen
5 store
6 bath/shower/toilet
7 toilets
8 clean linen
9 cleaner
10 quiet room
11 day area/OT
12 servery
13 medecines
14 sluice/dirty linen
15 sister
16 interview
17 clinical
18 4 bed room
19 2 bed room
20 day room

The top floor at the Maudsley District centre. It provides for three levels of care: low dependency in single bedrooms of domestic character; high supervision in four-bed rooms with day space, a room for occupational therapy and a kitchen for serving meals to patients who cannot go to the main dining room on the floor below; and intensive supervision in two-bed rooms whose occupants share a small dayroom which gives access to an inner suite of single rooms for patients who need to be segregated. By opening or closing interconnecting doors the degree of movement between these zones can be controlled according to the types and severity of illness being treated. Architects: Architects' Co-Partnership

various daily activities, craft rooms or manual and clerical workshops, rooms for laundry, ironing and hairdressing, for withdrawal or quiet reading, one or more classrooms, a dining room and kitchen, perhaps with facilities for a few patients to do their own preparation, cooking and washing-up. There should be a few discussion rooms for groups of about a dozen, and rooms where doctors and other staff can work and talk with three or four other people. A large space is likely to be needed for meetings, parties or entertainments attended by everybody using the building. There may be a need for a creche or nursery.

If the centre includes beds, some of these are likely to be arranged similarly to those in a psychiatric ward. For patients of minimum dependency accommodation may well be in single rooms of a hostel type more akin to student study-bedrooms, a few rooms being large enough to take a mother and child.

Some of the patients may be in the building both day and night, others may come only for the day or part of the day, and others may come only in the evenings and to sleep. If the centre caters for this sort of mixed occupancy it may be necessary to plan so that some of the daytime areas can be shut off easily and naturally in the evening; this will avoid residents straying into unsupervised parts of the building.

Mental handicap

A distinction must be made between the nature of the services and accommodation appropriate for the mentally ill and those needed for the mentally handicapped. The mentally ill are generally curable to some degree and the cure may involve different forms of continued support for differing periods of time; they present a range of problems and there is a range of ways for dealing with them.

Those patients who are variously defined as mentally subnormal, handicapped or retarded constitute a different category, in which the development of the mind is incomplete or arrested and the capacity for learning severely limited. Mental handicap is also sometimes associated with physical disability and sometimes with behaviour disturbance.

The purpose of care is not so much to enable patients to return to normal society as to attempt to help them to develop to the greatest extent possible such rudimentary skills as they possess. This includes providing assistance in the tasks of everyday living such as washing, dressing and eating, speech and movement, and teaching simple crafts and skills that can do something to enrich the quality of the life they can lead. This can help to relieve the burden on their families or on the health and social services that have to look after them.

Relatively few of the mentally handicapped are incapable of learning anything. Most can be taught to look after themselves to some degree and many can achieve simple occupations which are useful. In all societies some mentally handicapped people, whether children or adults, live with their families, but there will always be some whose families cannot sustain the burden continuously or who have no family to support them.

Legislation in Britain uses the term 'subnormal' for the mentally handicapped who need special care and training and 'severely sub-normal' for those needing protection. The World Health Organisation and the USA use the term 'mental retardation' and classify it as 'mild', 'moderate', 'severe' or 'profound'.

In terms of appropriate buildings, however, the mentally handicapped can be considered in three main groups: first, the severely handicapped who depend on almost continuous attention; second, those who although less severely handicapped need fairly constant help; and third, those whose handicap is less severe and who in many cases are capable of being found a place in society but may need sheltered occupation and housing. In this chapter we deal principally with design for the first two groups, as these are the ones with which the hospital and health services will be primarily concerned.

Residential homes for the mentally handicapped

Today's approach is the antithesis of the huge and intimidating asylum, with its atmosphere of a gaol. The aim is for small institutions, broken down into units of domestic character. In these surroundings most of the patients can usually be trained to identify themselves with such places and to perform simple basic domestic activities. The staff can work in congenial surroundings, which relieves some of the considerable strain to which they are exposed. Unlike the remote asylum, on which society has turned its back, these small units will be sited whenever possible in places where they are in touch with the community.

Opinions differ, but it is probably true to say that much current thinking today would restrict the size of new residential accommodation for the mentally handicapped to between 100 and 200 beds at the very most. However, it is recognised in the UK and elsewhere that conditions cannot be changed rapidly without a massive financial injection. This means the inherited building stock of the large old institutions, and their occupants, will remain with us for some time

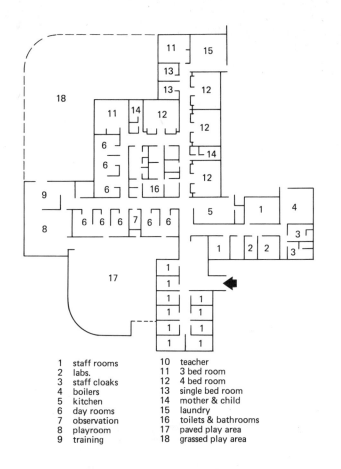

Hilda Lewis House, a residential unit for mentally handicapped children at the Bethlem Royal Hospital, Beckenham, Kent. Designed to accommodate twenty-four children, some of them long stay, the main purpose of the unit was to carry out research into their treatment and care. The residential part of the building consists of a central toilet area (for reasons of incontinence) with bedrooms and dayrooms grouped around it. The dayrooms are separated by sliding screens to allow flexibility of groupings. Architects: Grahame Herbert Associates

1	staff rooms	10	teacher
2	labs.	11	3 bed room
3	staff cloaks	12	4 bed room
4	boilers	13	single bed room
5	kitchen	14	mother & child
6	day rooms	15	laundry
7	observation	16	toilets & bathrooms
8	playroom	17	paved play area
9	training	18	grassed play area

The playroom at Hilda Lewis House, which opens on to a paved play area behind the wall in the foreground

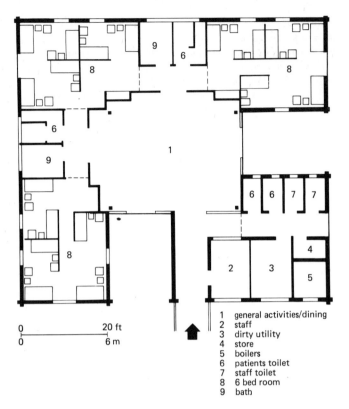

0   6 m

1   general activities/dining
2   staff
3   dirty utility
4   store
5   boilers
6   patients toilet
7   staff toilet
8   6 bed room
9   bath

A unit designed to be linked to existing facilities at Northfields Hospital. It is for severely mentally handicapped people, all of whom have great difficulties of mobility and most of whom are in wheelchairs. Three six-bed spaces cluster round a central dining and general activity area off which are the staff and ancillary rooms. Meals are trolleyed from the main building and there is no separate servery. Each bed has its own corner, the island ones formed by low screens, and all patient's spaces have direct access to the open air. Architects: Derek Stow and Partners

A unit at Northfields Hospital, showing the link to existing buildings

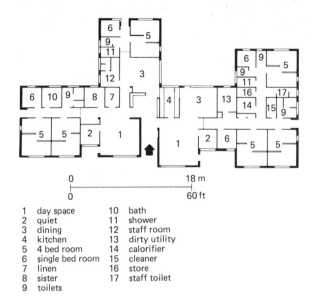

1 day space
2 quiet
3 dining
4 kitchen
5 4 bed room
6 single bed room
7 linen
8 sister
9 toilets
10 bath
11 shower
12 staff room
13 dirty utility
14 calorifier
15 cleaner
16 store
17 staff toilet

An adult residential unit for the mentally handicapped at Chase Farm Hospital, Enfield, housing two groups of fourteen residents, each with day spaces and dining areas. There are five residential units for adults, two for children, and a day centre

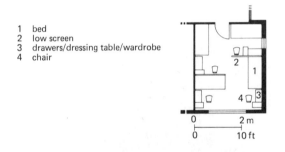

1 bed
2 low screen
3 drawers/dressing table/wardrobe
4 chair

Typical bedroom arrangement at Chase Farm Hospital. Each adult bed is in a corner, with its own storage for clothes and personal belongings. Architects: Stillman and Eastwick-Field

to come, however much we would like to be able to do without them. Even with present restrictions on capital expenditure much can be done with existing buildings.

The aim is to reduce their overcrowding, to break them down into smaller nursing units, and to increase their amenities without adding unduly to their physical size. In parallel with this, new provisions tend to be in the form of residential homes that are domestic in conception, some of them small and local enough for the handicapped to be cared for reasonably near their families. It is in this direction that the most interesting developments have taken place in recent years.

For those who have to leave their family but do not need the special medical or nursing care that a hospital provides the British government paper of 1971, '*Better Services for the Mentally Handicapped*',

envisaged small residential homes, usually for residents of both sexes. These would house twenty-five adults or twenty children (but many of them less than this) where staff and residents could become a substitute family group. It was considered that most of the adults should have single bedrooms and that no rooms should contain more than four beds.

Health and local authorities have responded to the concept of residential homes in different ways. Although most people are agreed that large institutions are undesirable, the problem is how to organise care for large numbers of people when only relatively small resources are available.

To some extent size may depend upon the degree of handicap. At one end of the scale accommodation has been provided in only slightly modified houses of truly domestic size, either specially built or converted for the purpose, closely integrated with an existing community. At the other end of the scale larger and more self-sufficient establishments have been constructed, centred around more specialised facilities. Although composed of 'houses' of relatively domestic size these units nevertheless have some of the characteristics of the large establishment, albeit in a more humane form. The fact that their architectural character strives to avoid the traditional atmosphere of an 'institution', sometimes successfully, does not necessarily neutralise the organisational regimes that their administrative conception implies.

The larger residential homes for adults provide about 100 beds, with a central place for day care that may serve, in addition, a few handicapped people from the district, and with nearby residential accommodation for staff. Whilst many people would prefer to restrict living units to between six and eight handicapped people there seems little doubt that the basic residential groups should not exceed about twelve; in some cases two 'houses' for groups of this size are joined to share a kitchen.

Because physical disability is a major constraint, the house for each group is generally on one floor only, with access to garden space outside. The building is arranged as normally as circumstances permit around a comfortable living room and dining area, with bedrooms containing from one to four beds. They aim to be domestic in character, with storage for personal belongings, and to be generously planned with easily accessible bathrooms and toilets. Units of this nature are linked to a centre for day care, and it is accepted that it is desirable that the handicapped should move to such a centre daily rather than have everything artificially at hand within a single building, as happens in so many institutions. Detailed planning must recognise the requirements imposed by the wheelchair and that some of the residents, although

111

1 single bed
2 wash/toilet
3 disposal
4 4 bed
5 store
6 living area
7 dining
8 kitchen
9 rest room
10 waiting
11 cleaner
12 office

0 ——————— 18 m
0 ——————— 60 ft

One of four residential buildings for mentally handicapped adults at Lightwood House, Norton, Sheffield. Each building is divided into two 'houses' for twelve people, sharing a kitchen. Covered ways link the residential buildings to a fifteen place Day Centre: this is arranged around a large social area with facilities for training in physical mobility, and contains suites of inter-communicating teaching spaces, a central kitchen, consultants' rooms and administration. Architects: Hutchinson, Locke and Monk

The central social area at Lightwood House, lofty enough to permit climbing equipment, showing the link to the teaching spaces and residential buildings. (Photo: Richard Bryant)

The Day Centre at Lightwood House. The main social area opens on to a terrace and green. Administration and consultants' rooms are on the left, teaching spaces and the link to the residential buildings on the right. (Photo: Richard Bryant)

A teaching space at Lightwood House. (Photo: Richard Bryant)

not chairbound, will at times need the assistance of another person to perform quite simple activities. Designers must also take account of the considerable difficulties presented by incontinence, which demand adequate and strategically placed toilets and showers, and pose special problems in the selection of finishes and methods of cleaning.

The function of a day centre in such a community is both social and educational, and is likely to be combined with administration and a central kitchen. It will include craft rooms and a laundry available to residents and day patients from the district. Its principal space, around which the life of the centre may well revolve, will probably be a major area equipped with gymnastic apparatus for physical activities and physiotherapy. This area can also be used for social functions, entertainments, parties and dances.

In the UK there have been experiments that provide care in even smaller residential units and rely to a lesser extent on centralised activities and institutionalised arrangements. There are examples of units

for about eight adults, arranged around a living room and dining room, with a kitchen and utility room planned on the assumption that the household will prepare some of its own meals and do its own housework, and that to as great an extent as possible residents and staff will function as a family that lives, works and eats together. Units on this scale, which can be aggregated if local needs demand it, are more likely to be able to provide care that is geographically close to the family of the mentally handicapped and to offer opportunities for a more normal relationship with the local community.

The severely handicapped can behave in ways that can be extremely disturbing, making great demands on the people who look after them. Although staff numbers may be high the staff are often faced with situations which are very difficult to contain. The planning of residential units must take this into account, particularly if the category of residents is likely to give rise frequently to disruptive behaviour that will communicate itself to others and get out of hand. Open plans of both work and living areas need

Residential unit for forty-eight mentally handicapped adults at Boston, Lincolnshire, comprising two residential buildings for patients, a day care centre planned to accommodate in addition sixteen patients from the neighbourhood, and ten separate staff houses. Garden walls separate the patients' territory from the staff and public areas. Architects' Co-Partnership

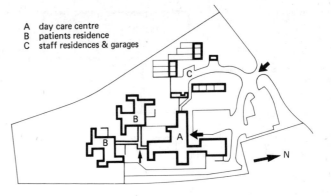

A day care centre
B patients residence
C staff residences & garages

One of the two residential buildings for twenty-four patients at Boston. It is divided into two social groups of twelve, each with its own living and eating area but sharing a kitchen/servery. Bedroom areas are further sub-divided into units of six, with their own sanitary accommodation and linen storage. All bedroom units and living areas have access to sheltered courtyards, and the building is linked to the day care centre by an enclosed walkway

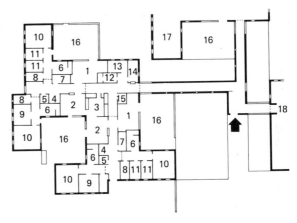

1	living room	10	4 bed room
2	dining/activity	11	single bed room
3	kitchen	12	cloaks
4	wheelchairs	13	staff room
5	toilet	14	office
6	bath, shower & toilet	15	cleaner
7	disposal	16	courtyard
8	linen	17	patients residence
9	2 bed room	18	day care centre

The day care centre at Boston. Four wings relate to the central entrance hall and activity space: one for visitors, administration, consultation and treatment, a second for kitchen and staff amenities, a third for relatively heavy or noisy industrial and woodworking therapy, and a fourth, which leads to the patients' residential accommodation, for education and light occupational therapy. Residents have meals in their own buildings, trolleyed from the kitchen. Day patients eat in the dining room off the central activity space. Architects: Architects' Co-Partnership

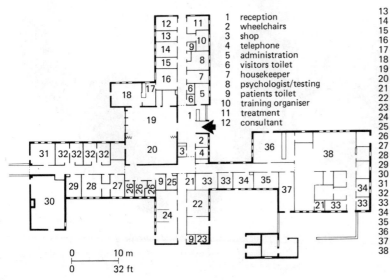

1	reception	13	interview
2	wheelchairs	14	seminar
3	shop	15	nursing administration
4	telephone	16	domestic training
5	administration	17	kitchen
6	visitors toilet	18	day patients dining
7	housekeeper	19	social area
8	psychologist/testing	20	locomotion/adventure
9	patients toilet	21	cleaner
10	training organiser	22	joinery & store
11	treatment	23	dirty linen
12	consultant	24	industrial therapy
		25	disposal
		26	patients toilet/bath or shower
		27	dressmaking
		28	basketwork
		29	pottery
		30	boilers
		31	education
		32	individual tuition/therapy
		33	staff change
		34	staff room
		35	staff coffee/sandwiches
		36	staff dining
		37	housekeeping store
		38	kitchen

115

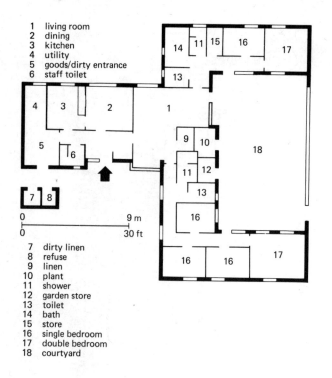

1 living room
2 dining
3 kitchen
4 utility
5 goods/dirty entrance
6 staff toilet

0 _____ 9 m
0 _____ 30 ft

7 dirty linen
8 refuse
9 linen
10 plant
11 shower
12 garden store
13 toilet
14 bath
15 store
16 single bedroom
17 double bedroom
18 courtyard

A house plan for the mentally handicapped in South West Wales. Each house is for eight residents. A variety of single and double bedded rooms or three bedded spaces divided by screens is possible, centred on their own day time accommodation and with access to a courtyard. All meals are served in the house. Breakfast and evening meals are made in the kitchen and staff and patients eat and wash up together whenever possible. Patients are encouraged to do their own laundry in the utility room. Architect: W. H. Simpson, Welsh Health Technical Services Organisation, Welsh Hospital Board

A group of three houses shown on the above plan. These single storey domestic buildings are situated as part of the community, on hospital sites in towns. Standard house plans can be combined in various ways to produce layouts enclosing sheltered courtyards. Each site houses about thirty-two patients and incorporates a therapy room which also serves as a community hall.

The entrance to a house for the mentally handicapped, South West Wales

rigorous scrutiny from this point of view. In the case of the most severely handicapped, a disturbance can spread like wildfire. It may thus be desirable to be able to contain small numbers of residents in separate spaces where one or more members of staff can shut the door and deal with a situation before it infects a larger group.

Whether care is in the hands of nurses or, as some people now suggest, of residential care staff, looking after the mentally handicapped is probably the most demanding of all forms of 'nursing'. It is also inevitable that it requires a very high ratio of staff to handicapped residents. For this reason it is arguable that very small and self-contained domestic units, for all their virtue, may present problems when staff is difficult to recruit, train and retrain (as it is in all branches of medicine, whether in the developed or the developing world).

Although a one-to-one ratio of staff may be desirable for the most severely subnormal patients it is not usually possible to provide this degree of attention. Both for this category and for the less severely handicapped it is generally necessary to stretch resources further. Because the small and virtually independent 'family' house may present problems in this respect there are likely to be practical advantages if such small domestic units are related in a way that allows staff to be shared between them to some degree without the units losing their own identities.

If staff have the opportunity of sharing the territories of adjacent units and of acquiring some personal knowledge of adjoining residents it should make staff movement between one unit and another easier and more effective in an emergency, or when there is some temporary hiatus in staff numbers.

Bibliography

Abel-Smith, B., *The National Health Service: the first thirty years*, HMSO,London (1978)

Allen, R. W. & Karolyi, I., *Hospital planning handbook*, John Wiley & Sons, New York (1976)

Baasher, Carstairs, Giel & Hassler (ed.), *Mental health services in developing countries: papers at a seminar in Addis Ababa 1973*, WHO Offset No 22, WHO, Geneva (1975)

Baker, G. & Bevan, J., *A bibliography on health centres in the UK* Update Publications, London (1973)

Baker, Llewelyn-Davies, Sivadon, *Psychiatric services and architecture*, WHO, Geneva(1959)

Baynes, Ken (ed.), *Hospital research and briefing problems*, King Edward's Hospital Fund, London (1971)

Beales, J. G., *Sick health centres*, Pitman Medical, London (1978)

Bennett, A. E. (ed.), *Community hospitals: progress in development and evaluation*, Oxford Regional Hospital Board (1974)

Bridgman, R. F., *The rural hospital*, WHO Monograph No 22, WHO, Geneva (1955)

Cammock, Ruth, *Health centres handbook*, Borough of Newham and Medical Architecture Research Unit, Northern Polytechnic, London (1973)

Conference of Missionary Societies, *A model health centre: working party report by 1972 Medical Committee*, Conference of Missionary Societies in Great Britain and Ireland, London (1975)

Department of Health & Social Security, *Health centres: a design guide*, HMSO, London (1971)

Department of Health & Social Security, *Better services for the mentally handicapped*, HMSO, London (1971)

Department of Health & Social Security, *Better services for the mentally ill*, HMSO, London (1975)

Gainsborough, H. & J., *Principles of hospital design*, Architectural Press, London (1964)

Gish, Oscar, *Guidelines for health planners: the planning and management of health services in developing countries*, Tri-Med Books, London (1977)

Holroyd, W. A. H. (ed.), *Hospital traffic and supply problems*, King Edward's Hospital Fund, London (1968)

Institute of Health Service Administrators, *The Hospitals and Health Services Year Book*, The Institute of Health Service Administrators, London (1979)

King, Maurice, *Medical care in developing countries: a primer on the medicine of poverty*, Oxford University Press, Nairobi (1966)

Llewelyn-Davies, R. & Macaulay, H. M. C., *Hospital planning and administration*, WHO, Geneva (1966)

M.A.R.U., *Ward evaluation: St Thomas' Hospital*, Medical Architecture Research Unit, Northern Polytechnic, London (1977)

Merrison, Sir Alec (Chairman), *Report of the Royal Commission on the National Health Service*, HMSO, London (1979)

Mills, Alden B., *Functional planning of general hospitals*, McGraw-Hill, New York (1969)

Mills, E. D. (ed.), *Planning: Buildings for health, welfare and religion*, Butterworths, London (1976)

Newell, K. (ed.), *Health by the people*, WHO, Geneva (1975)

Nuffield Provincial Hospitals Trust, *Studies in the functions and design of hospitals*, Oxford University Press, London (1955)

Nuffield Provincial Hospitals Trust, *Central sterile supply: principles and practice*, Oxford University Press, London (1963)

Oxford Regional Hospital Board, *Evaluation of a deep ward plan* , Oxford Regional Hospital Board (1970)

Pütsep, Ervin, *Planning of surgical centres*, Lloyd-Luke, London (1973)

Pütsep, Ervin, *Modern Hospital: International planning practices*, Lloyd-Luke, London (1979)

Scottish Home & Health Department, *Health centres in Scotland: a design guide*, HMSO, Edinburgh (1973)

Terry, W. G. & McLaren, J. W., *Planning a diagnostic radiology department*, W. B. Saunders, London (1973)

Thompson, J. D. & Goldin, G., *The Hospital: a social and architectural history*, Yale University Press, London (1975)

Wingate, P., *The Penguin Medical Encyclopedia*, Harmondsworth (1976)

World Health Organisation, *Organisation of mental health services in developing countries*. Technical Report No 564, WHO, Geneva (1975)

World Health Organisation, *Approaches to the planning and design of health care facilities in Developing Areas*. WHO Offset Nos 29, 37, 45, WHO, Geneva (1976/7/9)

YRM International, *Health buildings in hot climates: a design guide for Thermal performance*, DHSS, London (1976)

Index